M. Bruhn

Mode

An Introc
Foreign Students

Part I

Modern Arabic

An Introductory Course for Foreign Students

Part I

by

Samar Attar

Librairie du Liban

Librairie du Liban
Riad Solh Square, Beirut.
Associated companies, branches and representatives throughout the world.

Reprinted 1997

Printed in Lebanon by
TYPOPRESS, Beirut

TABLE OF CONTENTS

PREFACE

TO THE STUDENT: Five questions you are likely to ask about the learning of Arabic.

1. WHY SHOULD I LEARN ARABIC?

1.1. THE LANGUAGE OF THE ARAB WORLD

1.1.1. Arabic is spoken by about 160 million people. It is the language of the Arab World, comprising the countries of North Africa, the Fertile Crescent of the Middle East, the Arab Peninsula and the Gulf States. Arabic is also spoken by large numbers of emigrés in communities all over the world.

1.1.2. The geopolitical importance of the Arab World is more evident today than ever before. Because of its oil wealth and its strategically important position between Eastern and Western hemispheres, as well as the unresolved Palestinian issue, the Arab World is a prominent focus for international concern.

1.2. THE LANGUAGE OF ISLAM

Arabic is used by the 600 million Moslems all over the world as the liturgical language of Islam.

1.3. ARABIC INFLUENCE ON ENGLISH

There are about 1,000 main words of Arabic origin in the English language and very many other words derived from Arabic. Arabic words can be found in every area of language use, ranging from the sciences to the arts, to foods and other areas of everyday life.

1.4. ARABIC AS THE LANGUAGE OF CULTURE AND CIVILIZATION IN THE MIDDLE AGES

During the Middle Ages (the 8th to 13th centuries) the Arabic speaking peoples were the main bearers of the torch of civilization. Arabic was the medium through which the science and philosophy of Greece and other ancient civilizations were recovered, supplemented and transmitted in such a way as to make possible the European Renaissance.

1.5. Arabic at the United Nations

Arabic is one of the official working languages at the United Nations.

2. What kind of Arabic will I be learning?

It is important that the student realizes from the start that there are two kinds of Arabic:

1. One is spoken at home, or in the street, but it is not written.
2. The second is spoken in schools and universities, in radio and television, and is written in newspapers and books. It is this language that the student will be learning here.

   The language used in this book is Modern Standard Arabic, which, unlike the various dialects, whether Syrian-Lebanese or Egyptian, enables the student to be understood eveywhere in the Arab World. Thus, the dialogues of the fifteen lessons are close to but not identical with colloquial Arabic.

3. What will I learn by the end of this course?

3.1. General Aim

The course is an introduction to Arabic for students with no previous knowledge of the language. It is designed as part of a sequence that will enable the student to understand, speak, read and write Modern Standard Arabic with ease.

3.2. Specific Objectives

3.2.1. The student should be able to comprehend and to summarize the basic information (ideas, arguments, themes, issues) of almost any modern Arabic text, whether printed or spoken.

3.2.2. To take part in simple but also serious conversations with educated Arabs, to reproduce and appropriately modify patterns of simple spoken Arabic.

3.2.3. To read through and understand written texts of moderate difficulty.

3.2.4. To write simple but correct and accurate Arabic.

3.2.5. To gain an insight through the study of exemplary texts into the political and cultural history of the Arabs.

4. How will I gain an insight into the history and civilization of the Arabs?

The material of the dialogues all deal in one way or another with one Arab city, Damascus. There is a continuous "red thread" provided by the perspective of John, an American student, who comes to Syria to study Arabic at Damascus University. Chapters dealing with travel and tourism (arrival at the airport, going to the bank, museum, post office) are complemented by discussion on topical questions of general interest presented from a student's point of view (university life, the position of women in the city, students' interests in politics and the arts, aspects of the political turmoil in the Middle East) and by a treatment of more specific socio-cultural and historical developments (Old and New Damascus, economic development). In contrast to the dialogues, the comprehension texts at the end of each chapter feature a description of various topics of life experiences in other Arab cities or countries, respectively: Lesson 4 deals with the Lebanese ritual of Māzza, Lesson 6 with the Egyptian museum in Cairo, Lesson 7 describes the mosques of Karbala in Iraq, as well as the "theatre" conventions of the Shiite Moslems, Lesson 11 centers on the topic of "politics and the cinema" by briefly discussing two films, **Battle of Algiers** and **Circle of Deceit.**

In general, the texts move gradually from concrete situations to a more abstract treatment of socio-cultural issues. As a result, the student will be able to gain insights into selected areas of the political and cultural life of the Arabs. To complement this aspect of the course, it is suggested that groups of students work together on projects to provide additional information according to their specific interests. Their source material, however, need not be in Arabic. A language book cannot, of course, offer a complete course in civilization. The material in this book provides exemplary texts; thus the information on the city of Damascus is meant only as a model which could be easily substituted by other Arab cities. Similarly, all the material in the book could and, indeed, should be augmented with a variety of texts and integrated into the course.

5. Is Arabic a difficult language?

Unfortunately, the answer must be "Yes." It goes without saying that native speakers of English find learning Arabic a more daunting task than learning German or French. On the other hand, it is certainly not impossible, and many students have found it a very rewarding experience. It can - and should - also be fun, especially if the approach chosen is oriented towards quick progress in communicative skills, as is the case in this book. Furthermore, there are ways to overcome the specific difficulties inherent in studying Arabic.

5.1. The first difficulty that a student will encounter in learning Arabic is hearing or reproducing certain sounds. It is essential that a student should listen to the tapes which accompany this book and attempt to reproduce the sounds as frequently as possible. These tapes will be produced soon.

5.2. The second difficulty is writing. Arabic has a very different alphabet from Latin. Letters have different forms, at the beginning, middle or end of a word. To complicate things still more, short vowels are not written. In order to overcome this difficulty, the student is encouraged to write and rewrite texts and exercises and make sure that he or she knows not only how to say something by heart and how to read it, but how to write it as well. Writing always goes hand in hand with reading and hearing; continued practice is essential.

5.3. The third difficulty, which is not necessarily peculiar to Arabic, is how to reach a level of fluency that allows students to conduct a simple conversation. The best way to overcome this difficulty is to **memorize** right from the beginning a variety of useful expressions, and to practise the use of various conversational patterns (e.g., when learning: "Do you have a lecture?" you should automatically be able to summon to your mind everything you learned that could be used with "Do you have...," or when you learn "Could I see him tonight?" you should be able to vary this pattern accordingly: "Could I see her tomorrow, or after tomorrow?" etc. Paying attention to these patterns, right from the beginning, will help you a great deal in expressing yourself with ease).

5.4. An important key in comprehending new texts lies in identifying the roots of Arabic words, a practice the student should familiarize himself/herself from the very beginning of his-her course. The roots of vocabulary are required to check items in the dictionary, and they allow the comprehension of passages through an identification of word fields, cognates and the context in which vocabulary items appear. One cannot find the word 'bank' simply under 'bank' as in English dictionaries. Thus, when the student learns the verb صرف (he changed 'money'), s/he should understand that under this item words like

صرّاف ـ صيارفة (money-changer, -s),
مصرف ـ مصارف (bank, -s) etc.,

appear in the Arabic dictionary. Therefore, it is always advisable to learn the root of certain words, and to try to group these words together.
Don't study "he wrote" كتب by itself. Always remember the following:

He wrote/writes (writing)	كتب ـ يكتب (كتابة)
Writer/s masc.	كاتب ـ كتّاب
Writer/s fem.	كاتبة ـ كاتبات

Book/s	كتاب ـ كتب
Written; letter/s	مكتوب ـ مكاتيب
Library/ies	مكتبة ـ مكتبات
Office/s	مكتب ـ مكاتب

and so on.

If the student pays attention to the roots of Arabic words right from the beginning of the course, intelligent guesses become possible when the student is confronted with a new text.

This book has taken a very long time to write. In a sense, it goes back as far as 1972 when I first taught Arabic in an intensive summer program at the Monterey Institute of International Studies in Monterey, California. Since then I taught Arabic in West Germany, and Australia. Everywhere, I had intelligent, motivated students who enjoyed learning the language as much as I did teaching them. They invariably found the course a lot of fun; occassional moments of frustration not withstanding. I wrote the book thinking of all these students, but particularly the group in Monterey 1972-73 and among them Taylor C. who spent the summer sleeping in his old station wagon because he had paid a lot of money on tuition and he hadn't enough to pay rent. We had a great time together. I wish all of you using this book as much success as Taylor, without the nightly discomfort naturally, and I hope you too will find learning Arabic a stimulating and enjoyable experience as he did.

THE ARABIC ALPHABET

Name of the letter	Beginning of the word	Middle of the word	End of the word	Alone	Translitera-tion	Pronunciation
ألف 'alif	ا	ـا	ـا	ا	ā	same as father
همزة hamza (Alif acts as the bearer of Hamza which sits on the top or bottom of Alif)				أَ أُ إِ	' a,u,i	
باء bā'	بـ	ـبـ	ـب	ب	b	same sound as b: but, bit, book
تاء tā'	تـ	ـتـ	ـت	ت	t	same sound as t: tug, tick, took
(Also tā' marbūṭah as the final letter in a word)			ـة	ة	t	when vocalized tā', when not vocalized: a
ثاء t̲hā'	ثـ	ـثـ	ـث	ث	t̲h	same sound as the unvoiced th of English: thank, thing
جيم jīm	جـ	ـجـ	ـج	ج	j	same as j: jim, jam (in Egypt same as g: get)
حاء ḥā'	حـ	ـحـ	ـح	ح	ḥ	no equivalent (an emphatic 'h' pronounced with a strong expulsion of the breath)

Name of the letter	Beginning of the word	Middle of the word	End of the word	Alone	Translitera-tion	Pronunciation
خاء khā’	خـ	ـخـ	ـخ	خ	kh	same as German: ach, Bach, Buch
دال dāl	د	ـد	ـد	د	d	same as d: dog, dig, dug
ذال dhāl	ذ	ـذ	ـذ	ذ	dh	same as the voiced th of English: thus, this
راء rā’	ر	ـر	ـر	ر	r	rolled r: road
زاي zāy	ز	ـز	ـز	ز	z	same as z: zoo
سين sīn	سـ	ـسـ	ـس	س	s	same as s: Sam, sin
شين shīn	شـ	ـشـ	ـش	ش	sh	same as sh: sham, shame, sheep
صاد ṣād	صـ	ـصـ	ـص	ص	ṣ	no equivalent (an emphatic ‘s’ pronounced with the teeth slightly apart pressing the tip of the tongue against the lower teeth)
ضاد ḍād	ضـ	ـضـ	ـض	ض	ḍ	no equivalent (an emphatic ‘d’ pronounced with the tongue pressing against the edge of the upper teeth with the tip protruding)

Name of the letter	Beginning of the word	Middle of the word	End of the word	Alone	Transliteration	Pronunciation
طاء ṭā’	طـ	ـطـ	ـط	ط	ṭ	no equivalent: emphatic ṭ. You should be able to bite the sides of the tongue with the molars. Keep your tongue as flat as possible.
ظاء ẓā’	ظـ	ـظـ	ـظ	ظ	ẓ	also no equivalent: emphatic ẓ.
عين ‘ayn	عـ	ـعـ	ـع	ع	‘	no equivalent (pronounced with constriction of the larynx)
غين gẖayn	غـ	ـغـ	ـغ	غ	gẖ	no equivalent. Close to German: **Rand, Rind** and **rund.** Also close to the Parisian r. (the sound of gargling)
فاء fā’	فـ	ـفـ	ـف	ف	f	same as f: fund, fig, far
قاف qāf	قـ	ـقـ	ـق	ق	q	no equivalent: a k pronounced as far back in the throat as possible.
كاف kāf	كـ	ـكـ	ـك	ك	k	same as k: kind, Canada

Name of the letter	Beginning of the word	Middle of the word	End of the word	Alone	Translitera-tion	Pronunciation
لام lām	لـ	ـلـ	ـل	ل	l	same as l: lung, lib, lad
ميم mīm	مـ	ـمـ	ـم	م	m	same as m: mum, mid, mad
نون nūn	نـ	ـنـ	ـن	ن	n	same as n: nun, Nick, nap
هاء hā’	هـ	ـهـ	ـه, ة	ه	h	same as h: hub, hiss, hook
واو wāw (Wāw acts as the bearer of Hamza)	و	ـو ـؤ	ـو	و	w (ū, au, aw)	same as wadi, wood, with, (woo, Mauritania, approximately how)
ياء yā’ (Ya acts as the bearer of Hamza)	يـ	ـيـ ـئـ	ـي ـىء	ي	y (ī,ay,ai)	same as y: yap, yippies, (bee, Ayub, rain)
Note: hamza alone on the line		ء	ء		’	a definite break in the voice as in a Cockney pronunciation of ‘t’ in butter, or bottle

UNIT I

1. Conversation

		Transliteration	
1-	Good morning	*Ṣabāḥa͜l-khayr*	١ ـ صباح الخير
	Good evening	*Masā'a͜l-khayr*	مساء الخير
2-	My name is ...	*Ismī ...*	٢ ـ اسمي . . .
	What is your name? (masc., sing.)	*Ma͜smuka?*	ما اسمكَ؟
	What is your name? (fem., sing.)	*Ma͜smuki?*	ما اسمكِ؟
3-	I am from...	*Anā min...*	٣ ـ أنا من . . .
	Where are you from? (masc., sing.)	*Min ayna anta?*	من أين أنتَ؟
	Where are you from? (fem., sing.)	*Min ayna anti?*	من أين أنتِ؟
4-	I am from...	*Anā min...*	٤ ـ أنا من . . .
	Syria	*Sūriya*	سوريّة
	Lebanon	*Lubnān*	لبنان
	Iraq	*Al-'irāq*	العراق

	Transliteration	
Palestine	*Filisṭīn*	فلسطين
Bahrain	*Al-Baḥrayn*	البحرين
Qatar	*Qaṭar*	قطر
Oman	*'umān*	عُمان
Kuwait	*Al-Kuwayt*	الكويت
Saudi Arabia	*As-Sa'ūdīya*	السعودية
Yemen	*Al-Yaman*	اليمن
Somalia	*Aṣ-Ṣūmāl*	الصومال
Sudan	*As-Sūdān*	السودان
Libya	*Lībyā*	ليبيا
Tunisia	*Tūnis*	تونس
Algeria	*Al-Jazā'ir*	الجزائر
Mauritania	*Maurītāniā*	موريتانيا
Egypt	*Miṣr*	مصر
Morocco	*Al-Maghrib*	المغرب
5- What are the Arab countries?	*Mā hiya͜d-duwalu͜l 'arabiya?*	٥ ـ ما هي الدول العربيّة؟
The Arab countries are…	*Ad-Duwalu͜l-'arabiyatu hiya…*	الدول العربيّة هي: . . .
6- I am from…	*Anā min…*	٦ ـ أنا من . . .
Asia	*Āsyā*	آسيا
Australia	*Ustrāliyā*	أستراليا

	Transliteration	
America	*Amrīka*	أمريكا
Europe	*(Urubbā, Awrubbā), Awruppā*	أوربّا
Africa	*Ifrīqyā*	إفريقيا

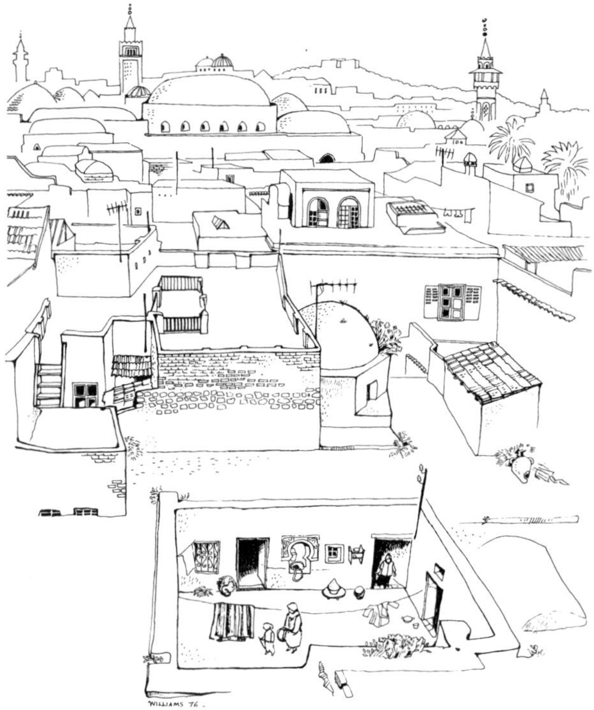

Tunis, (by Williams) تونس

7- I am from...	*Anā min...*	٧ ـ أنا من . . .
England	*Ingiltera*	إنكلترة
France	*Faransā*	فرنسا
Holland	*Hollandā*	هولندا
Italy	*Īṭālyā*	إيطاليا
Switzerland	*Swīsrā*	سويسرا
Spain	*Ispāniā, Isbāniā*	إسبانيا
Finland	*Finlandā*	فنلندا
	etc...	إلخ

Transliteration

		Transliteration	
8-	Zero	*Ṣifr*	٨ - صفر ٠
	One	*Wāḥid*	واحد ١
	Two	*Ithnān*	اثنان ٢
	Three	*Thalātha*	ثلاثة ٣
	Four	*Arba'a*	أربعة ٤
	Five	*Khamsa*	خمسة ٥
9-	So long	*Ila‿l-liqā'*	٩ - إلى اللقاء

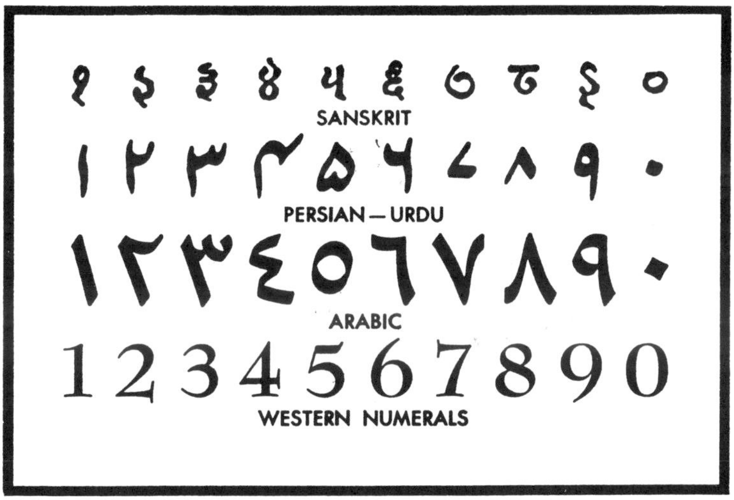

Sanskrit numerals from India, along with Persian-Urdu numerals used in Middle East, indicate how our Western numbers came to be. Western numbers are still called "Arabic numerals" because their shapes come from numbers used in Arab lands and Western mathematicians learned of the new numbers from Arabs. Western numbers did not begin to look as they do at left, until movable type for printing was invented during the fifteenth century.

The earliest form of the zero was invented in India about 500 A.D. It was the forerunner of one of the world's great discoveries. ✱ When the Indian, or Hindu, zero came to Baghdad in the ninth century, it was thought of merely as a dot meant to mark an empty space in a series of numbers. The dot was called **sunya,** meaning "empty" or "blank." ✱ Arab scholars saw that **sunya** was really another number which, when added to numbers 1 through 9, made it possible to compute in units of ten and to write all numbers with just 10 symbols – in contrast to the hundreds of symbols required by other numbering systems. The Greeks, for example, had to memorize 27 different symbols just to write the numbers 1 through 999, and the Roman numeral system was equally awkward. ✱ The nine "Arabic numerals," plus the zero, became the **place system** of numbers – the system that allows the nine basic symbols in different combinations to represent every possible quantity and assigns a different value to each symbol depending on its **place** or position in a series. In the number 999, for example, each nine has its own value: the left nine means 900; the middle nine means 90; and the right nine means nine. And the zeros in the numbers 900 and 90 fill the "empty" positions and reveal the values of the symbol 9. ✱ Despite the ease of the numbering system developed by the Arabs, Europeans persisted in using clumsy Roman numerals for centuries. Finally, in the thirteenth century, Arab teachers showed European mathematicians that the Arab system – with its nine symbols and all-important zero – worked best of all.

2. The non-connector letters

Arabic which is written from right to left has 28 consonants and 6 vowels. Unlike the Latin alphabet there are no capital letters, but many Arabic letters have various forms at the beginning, middle, or end of the words. There are two major groups of letters:

1. The non-connectors are letters which cannot be joined to following letters. They are six letters:

ا - د - ذ - ر - ز - و

Name of the letter	Beginning of the word	Middle of the word	End of the word	Alone	Translit-eration	Pronunciation
1. 'Alif	ا	ـا	ـا	ا	ā	same as father
2. Dāl	د	ـد	ـد	د	d	same as dad
					دادا	
3. Dhāl	ذ	ـذ	ـذ	ذ	dh	same as thus
					ذاذَ - إذا - آذار -	
4. Rā'	ر	ـر	ـر	ر	r	same as rolled Spanish 'r'
					رَدْ - دُرْ - دار	
5. Zāy	ز	ـز	ـز	ز	z	same as zoo
					زِر - زُرْ - زارَ - زادْ	

Name of the letter	Beginning of the word	Middle of the word	End of the word	Alone	Translit-eration	Pronunciation
6. Wāw	و	ـو	ـو	و	w	same as wasp
واوا - وِداد - وَز - وُد - وَدود - واد - وَرْد - راوَد					w	same as wasp
دود - زوْر - زُرْزور					ū	same as woo
دَوْر - رَوْد					aw	same as how
(Rose) روْز					au	same as Mauritania

2. The connectors are letters which must be joined to following letters. They constitute 22 letters of the alphabet.

3. Vowels

There are six vowels in Arabic: three long ones which are written, and three short ones which are not written except for the **Quran** and children's books where small marks representing the short vowels are placed above or below the consonant letters.

Short		Long	
ـَ	a	ا	aa
ـُ	u	و	uu
ـِ	i	ي	ii

4. Hamza

Hamza ـء is sometimes written over the 'alif أ. If its short vowel is ـَ 'a the letter أَ is pronounced 'a as in, أَنا 'anā (I am). If its short vowel is ـُ 'u the letter أُ is pronounced 'u as in أُستاذ 'ustaadh (a teacher). But if its short vowel is ـِ 'i the hamza is written under the alif إ, and the letter is pronounced 'i as in إقرأ Iqra' (read!).

5. Madda

The sign ـٓ over the alif is called مـدّة *madda* or 'lengthening'. When two *'alifs* in a word come together, then they are written ـٓ 'ā.e.g., القرآن al-qur'ān, the *Quran*, آمن 'āmana, he believed.

6. Sukūn

Note that the mark ـْ o placed above the letter is called *Sukūn* which indicates the absence of a vowel after a consonant. Example: دْ d.

7. Double Consonant, or Shadda

Shadda is represented by the sign ـّ which is written above the letter. Note the difference between: دَدَ and دَدَّ ، رَدَ and رَدَّ ، وَدَ and وَدَّ . The short vowel signs ـَ a and ـُ u are written over the ـّ while ـِ i is written under the ـّ— . Examples:

رَدِّ، أَوَدُّ، رَدَّ

8. Reading and dictation

1. The following examples contrast long ـا aa and short a ـَ.

Please read and write:

وَوَ	واوا	رَرَ	رارا	دَدَ	دادا
		زَزَ	زازا	ذَذَ	ذاذا

2. Contrast the long ū and short u:

رُزْ	روز	دُدْ	دود
زُزْ	زوز	ذُذْ	ذوذ

3. Read and write:

دا، دَ، دُ، دِ، دْ، دَّ، دُّ، دِّ

ذا، ذَ، ذُ، ذِ، ذْ، ذَّ، ذُّ، ذِّ

را، رَ، رُ، رِ، رْ، رَّ، رُّ، رِّ

زا، زَ، زُ، زِ، زْ، زَّ، زُّ، زِّ

وا، وَ، وُ، وِ، وْ، وَّ، وُّ، وِّ

9. Review: *Letters and Words*

دادا	sis (baby language)
ذادَ	he defended, protected
إذا	if
رَدّْ	reply
دُرّْ	pearls
دارْ	house
زِرّْ	button
رُزْ	rice
آذارْ	March
زارَ	he visited
زادْ	provisions
واوا	sick (baby language)
وِدادْ	friendship, also a woman's name

وَزّْ	geese
وُدّْ	affection, amity
وَدودْ	friendly
وادٍ	valley, river bed
وَرْدْ	roses
راوَدَ	he sought to tempt
دودْ	worms
زوْرْ	falsehood, untruth
زُرْزورْ	starling
دَوْرْ	role
رَوْدْ	exploration
روزْ	Rose (woman's name)

UNIT II

1. Conversation

	Transliteration	
1- Hello	*Marḥaban*	١ ـ مرحباً
	(Or marḥabā)	مرحبا
2- How are you? *(masc.,sing.)*	*Kayfa ḥāluka?*	٢ ـ كيف حالكَ؟
How are you? *(fem.,sing.)*	*Kayfa ḥāluki?*	كيف حالكِ؟
3- Thank you. And you? *(masc.,sing.)*	*Shukran. Al-ḥamdu li‿l-lāh. Wa anta?*	٣ ـ شكراً. الحمدلله. وأنتَ؟
And you? *(fem.,sing.)*	*Wa anti?*	وأنتِ؟
4- Where are you from? *(masc.,sing.)*	*Min ayna anta?*	٤ ـ من أين أنتَ؟
Where are you from? *(fem.,sing.)*	*Min ayna anti?*	من أين أنتِ؟
I am from Egypt	*Anā min miṣr*	أنا من مصر.
I am from Jordan	*Anā mina‿l-urdunn*	أنا من الأردنّ.
I am from Palestine	*Anā min filisṭīn*	أنا من فلسطين.

	I am from Morocco	*Anā mina‿l maghrib*	أنا من المغرب .
	I am from the United Arab Emirates	*Anā mina‿l imārāti‿l ‘arabiyati‿l muttaḥida*	أنا من الإمارات العربيّة المتّحدة .
	I am from North Yemen	*Anā mina‿l yamani‿sh shamāliya*	أنا من اليمن الشماليّة .
	I am from South Yemen	*Anā mina‿l yamani‿l janūbiya*	أنا من اليمن الجنوبيّة .
5-	Are you a student? *(masc.,sing.)*	*Hal anta ṭālibun? (or ṭālib)*	٥ - هل أنتَ طالب؟
	Yes. I am a student	*Na‘am. Anā ṭālibun (or ṭālib)*	نعم . أنا طالب .
6-	Are you a student? *(fem.,sing.)*	*Hal anti ṭālibatun? (or ṭāliba)*	٦ - هل أنتِ طالبة؟
	Yes. I am a student	*Na‘am. Anā ṭālibatun (or ṭāliba)*	نعم . أنا طالبة .

أنا طالِبة

7-	Where do you study? *(masc.,sing.)*	*Ayna tadrusu?*	٧ - أين تدرس؟
	I study at the university of…	*Adrusu fī jāmi‘ati…*	أدرس في جامعة . . .
8-	Where do you study? *(fem.,sing.)*	*Ayna tadrusīna?*	٨ - أين تدرسين؟
	I study at the university of…	*Adrusu fī jāmi‘ati…*	أدرس في جامعة . . .

9-	Six	*Sitta*	٩ - ستّة ٦
	Seven	*Sab'a*	سبعة ٧
	Eight	*T̲hamāniya*	ثمانية ٨
	Nine	*Tis'a*	تسعة ٩
	Ten	*'as̲hra*	عشرة ١٠

مع الأعداد

2. Nunation

The English indefinite article is a or an regardless whether the noun is a subject or an object. Examples:

1. **A student** lives next door.
2. I saw **a student** in the library.

In Arabic, the "n" sound indicates indefiniteness (which is called nunation) for both noun and adjective, but different vowels are added to indicate different cases. For example:

Nominative case	زِرٌّ	un
Genitive case	زِرٍّ	in
Accusative case	زِرًّا	an

Thus, the same Arabic nouns and adjectives are pronounced differently in different contexts because of their inflectional endings (un, in, and an).

NOTE At the end of a sentence or complete clause however, اً (an) may be pronounced as a long ā as in (marḥabā: hello), and the other case endings (un and in) not pronounced at all as in طالِبْ (ṭālib).

3. Reading and dictation

1. دودٌ (worms) ، دودٍ، دوداً

زِرٌّ (a button) ، زِرٍّ، زِرّاً

رَدٌّ (a reply) ، رَدٍّ، رَدّاً

وَزٌّ (geese) وَزٍّ، وَزّاً

2. زِرٌّ، وَزٌّ، رَدٌّ، دودٌ، دارٌ، دُرٌّ،

زادٌ، ودٌّ، وَرْدٌ، وَدودٌ، وداد

زِرًّا، وَزّاً، رُزّاً، رَدّاً،

دودٍ، دارٍ، دُرٍّ

ذَ، ذو، دُرٌّ، دارٌ

زِر، زارَ

تاجر - merchant

UNIT III

1. Conversation

Transliteration

1- Are you from Lebanon? *(masc.,sing.)*	*Hal anta min lubnān?*	١ ـ هل أنتَ من لبنان؟
No. I am from Jordan	*Lā. Anā mina‿l urdunn*	لا. أنا من الأردنّ.
Are you from… *(fem.,sing.)*	*Hal anti min…*	هل أنتِ من . . .
2- Are you from Africa? *(masc.,sing.)*	*Hal anta min ifrīqiyā?*	٢ ـ هل أنتَ من إفريقيا؟
No. I am from America	*Lā. Anā min amrīkā*	لا. أنا من أمريكا.
Are you from… *(fem.,sing.)*	*Hal anti min…*	هل أنتِ من . . .
3- Are you a student at London univesity?	*Hal anta ṭālibun fī jāmi'ati landon?*	٣ ـ هل أنتَ طالب في جامعة لندن؟
No. I am a student at Washington university	*Lā. Anā ṭālibun fī jāmi'ati wāshinṭun*	لا. أنا طالب في جامعة واشنطن.
Are you a student at… *(fem.,sing.)*	*Hal anti ṭālibatun fī…*	هل أنتِ طالبة في . . .

	No. I am a student at...	*Lā. Anā ṭālibatun fī...*	لا . أنا طالبة في . . .
4-	Are you a student? *(masc.,sing.)*	*Hal anta ṭālibun? (or ṭālib)*	٤ ـ هل أنتَ طالب؟
	No. I am a professor	*Lā. Anā ustāḏhun (or ustāḏh)*	لا . أنا أستاذ .
	Are you a student? *(fem.,sing.)*	*Hal anti ṭālibatun? (or ṭāliba)*	هل أنتِ طالبة؟

أنا أُستاذة

	No. I am a professor *(fem.,sing.)*	*Lā. Anā ustāḏhatun (or ustāḏha)*	لا . أنا أستاذة .
5-	What are the Arabic countries?	*Mā hiya͜d-duwalu͜l 'arabiyatu? (or arabiya)*	٥ ـ ما هي الدول العربية؟
	The Arabic countries are...	*Ad-Duwalu͜l 'arabiyatu hiya...*	الدول العربية هي : . . . .
6-	Are you Lebanese?	*Hal anta lubānī? (or lubnāniyun)*	٦ ـ هل أنتَ لبناني؟
	No. I am Syrian	*Lā. Anā sūrī (or sūriyun)*	لا . أنا سوري .
	Are you Egyptian? *(masc.,sing.)*	*Hal anta miṣrī?*	هل أنتَ مصري؟
	No. I am Palestinian *(masc.,sing.)*	*Lā. Anā filisṭīnī*	لا . أنا فلسطيني .
	Are you Tunisian? *(masc.,sing.)*	*Hal anta tūnisī?*	هل أنتَ تونسي؟

No. I am Mauritanian	*Lā. Anā mauritānī*	لا . أنا موريتاني .
Are you Iraqi? (masc., sing.)	*Hal anta 'irāqī?*	هل أنتَ عراقي ؟
No. I am Yemenite	*Lā. Anā yamanī*	لا . أنا يمني .
Are you Moroccan? (masc., sing.)	*Hal anta maghribī?*	هل أنتَ مغربي؟
No. I am Algerian	*Lā. Anā jazā'irī*	لا . أنا جزائري .
Are you Saudi? (masc., sing.)	*Hal anta sa'ūdī?*	هل أنت سعودي ؟
No. I am Jordanian	*Lā.Anā urdunī*	لا . أنا أردني .
Are you Palestinian? (fem., sing.)	*Hal anti filisṭīniya? (or filisṭīniyatun)*	هل أنتِ فلسطينية؟
No. I am Syrian	*Lā. Anā sūriya (or sūriyatun)*	لا . أنا سورية .
Are you Egyptian? (fem., sing.)	*Hal anti miṣriya?*	هل أنتِ مصرية؟
No. I am Lebanese (fem., sing.)	*Lā. Anā lubnāniya*	لا . أنا لبنانية .
Are you Saudi? (fem., sing.)	*Hal anti sa'ūdiya?*	هل أنتِ سعودية؟
No. I am Algerian	*Lā. Anā jazā'iriya*	لا . أنا جزائرية .

Note: At the end of a sentence or complete clause the case endings may be pronounced as in لُبْنانيٌّ lubnāniyun, or not pronounced at all as in لُبْناني lubnānī. The student should become aware of the two conventions, i.e., pronouncing words in their full form or in their pausal form. However, he/she should use one convention at a time.

7- What are the European countries?	*Mā hiya‿d-duwalu‿l awruppiyatu? (or awruppiya)*	٧ ـ ما هي الدول الأوربية؟
The European countries are...	*Ad-Duwalu‿l awrupiyatu hiya...*	الدول الأوربية هي :
England	*Ingiltrā*	إنكلترا

	France	*Faransā*	فرنسا
	Germany	*Almānyā*	ألمانيا
	Italy	*Īṭālyā*	إيطاليا
	Holland	*Hollandā*	هولندا
	Switzerland	*Swīsrā*	سويسرا
	Spain	*Ispānyā*	إسبانيا
	Russia	*Rūsyā*	روسيا
	(The Soviet Union)	*(Al-Ittiḥād as-sōvyātī)*	(الاتحاد السوفياتي)
	Sweden	*As-Suwayd*	السويد
	Yugoslavia	*Yūghoslāviā*	يوغسلافيا
	Poland	*Pōllandā*	بولندا
	Bulgaria	*Bulghāriyā*	بلغاريا
	Austria	*An-Nimsā*	النمسا
		etc...	إلخ . . .
8-	What are the Asian countries?	*Mā hiya‿d-duwalu‿l āsyawiyyatu? (or āsyawiyya)*	٨ ـ ما هي الدول الآسيوية؟
	India	*Al-Hind*	الهند
	China	*Aṣ-Ṣīn*	الصين
	Japan	*Al-Yābān*	اليابان
		etc...	إلخ . . .
9-	What are the African countries?	*Mā hiya‿d-duwalu‿l ifrīqiyatu? (or ifrīqiya)*	٩ ـ ما هي الدول الإفريقية؟
	Ghana	*Ghānā*	غانا

Nigeria	*Nījīryā*	نيجيريا
Kenya	*Kīnyā*	كينيا
	etc...	إلخ . . .
10- Are you English? *(masc.,sing.)*	*Hal anta inglīzī? (or inglīziyun)*	١٠ ـ هل أنتَ إنكليزي ؟
No. I am French	*Lā. Anā faransī*	لا . أنا فرنسي .
Are you German? *(masc.,sing.)*	*Hal anta almānī?*	هل أنتَ ألماني؟
No. I am Swede	*Lā. Anā suwīdī (suwaydī)*	لا . أنا سويدي .
Are you Spanish? *(masc.,sing.)*	*Hal anta ispānī?*	هل أنتَ إسباني؟
No. I am Russian	*Lā. Anā rūsī*	لا . أنا روسي .
Are you Ghanian? *(masc.,sing.)*	*Hal anta ghānī?*	هل أنتَ غاني؟
No. I am Nigerian	*Lā. Anā nījīrī*	لا . أنا نيجيري .
Are you Chinese? *(masc.,sing.)*	*Hal anta ṣīnī?*	هل أنتَ صيني ؟
No. I am Japanese	*Lā. Anā yābānī*	لا . أنا ياباني .
	etc...	إلخ . . .
Are you English? *(fem.,sing.)*	*Hal anti inglīziya? (or inglīziyatun)*	هل أنتِ إنكليزية؟
No. I am American	*Lā. Anā amrīkiya*	لا . أنا أمريكية .
	etc...	إلخ . . .

2. Five connector letters:

ب ـ ي ـ ن ـ ت ـ ه

The connectors are letters which must be joined to following letters. In this unit we will introduce five of these letters.

Name of the letter	Beginning of the word	Middle of the word	End of the word	Alone	Translit-eration	Pronunciation
1. Bā'	بـ	ـبـ	ـب	ب	b	same as but, book

Writing and reading:

بابا، بابٌ، دُبٌّ، رَبٌّ، بَرْدٌ، بارِدٌ، بارودٌ، بَرّادٌ.

Name of the letter	Beginning of the word	Middle of the word	End of the word	Alone	Translit-eration	Pronunciation
2. Yā'	يـ	ـيـ	ـي	ي	y (ī, ay, ai)	same as yippies (bee, Ayub, rain)

Writing and reading:

يَد	y	same as yap
وَزِيْر - رَبِّي - داري - زِرِّي - وَرْدي -	ī	same as bee
بَيْدَر - دَيْر	ay	same as bite

Name of the letter	Beginning of the word	Middle of the word	End of the word	Alone	Translit-eration	Pronunciation
3. Nūn	نـ	ـنـ	ـن	ن	n	same as now

Writing and reading:

نورٌ، نُوّار، نارٌ، بُنٌّ، بون، بَنون، دِيْن، بَيْنَ، بَيان.

Name of the letter	Beginning of the word	Middle of the word	End of the word	Alone	Translit-eration	Pronunciation
4. Tā'	تـ	ـتـ	ـت	ت	t	same as took

Writing and reading:

توت، تابوت، بَتَرَ، بَيْت.

Name of the letter	Beginning of the word	Middle of the word	End of the word	Alone	Translit-eration	Pronunciation
5. Hā'	هـ	ـهـ	ـه	ه	h	same as he

Writing and reading:

هُوَ، هِيَ، نَهار، بَهار، نَبيْه، هَذا، هَذِهِ

Note: Notice that the letter hā'(ه) is sometimes written with two dots above (ة, ـة) or a dash (ہ, ـہ) and pronounced "t" when it comes at the end of the word to denote the feminine ending of nouns and adjectives. This (ة) is called *Tā' Marbūta* (tied t). Example: رَبّة goddess.

3. Reading and dictation

دارُ هِنْد، ذَهَبَ نَبيه، هَرَبَتْ نُوّار، ذُباب، تيْه، بَنات، نَبي، بَهو، دَواب، بانَ، زادَ.

4. Review: letters and words

بابا	dad (baby language)
بابْ	door
دُبٌّ	bear
رَبٌّ	god
بَرْدْ	coldness
بارِدْ	cold
بارود	gunpowder
بَرّادْ	refrigerator
يَدْ	hand
وَزيرْ	minister
رَبّي	my god
داري	my house
زِرّي	my button
وَرْدي	my roses
بَيْدَرْ	threshing floor
دَيْرْ	convent
نورْ	light
نُوّارْ	blossom, also a woman's name

نارْ	fire
بُنٌّ	coffee beans
بون	Bonn
بَنونْ	sons, offsprings
ديْن	religion
بَيْنْ	between
بَيانْ	clearness
توتْ	mulberry
تابوتْ	coffin
بَتَرَ	he cut off
بَيْتْ	house
هُوَ	he
هِيَ	she
نَهارْ	day, daytime
بَهارْ	spice
نَبيه	eminent, distinguished, also a man's name
هَذا	this, masc.

هَذِهِ	this, fem.
دارُ هِنْد	Hind's house
ذَهَبَ نَبيه	Nabīh went
هَرَبَتْ نُوّار	Nuwwār fled
ذُبابْ	flies
تيه	wilderness
بَناتْ	daughters
نَبِي	prophet
بَهو	hall
دَواب	animals, riding animals
بانَ	something became evident, he came out
زادَ	he increased, grew

UNIT IV

1. Conversation

	Transliteration	
1- What country are you from? *(masc.,sing.)*	*Min ayyi baladin anta?*	١ - من أيّ بلد أنتَ؟
What country are you from? *(fem.,sing.)*	*Min ayyi baladin anti?*	من أيّ بلد أنتِ؟
I am from...	*Anā min...*	أنا من . . .
2- What city are you from? *(masc.,sing.)*	*Min ayyi madīnatin anta?*	٢ - من أيّ مدينة أنتَ؟
What city are you from? *(fem.,sing.)*	*Min ayyi madīnatin anti?*	من أيّ مدينة أنتِ؟
I am from the city of....	*Anā min madīnati...*	أنا من مدينة . . .
3- Beirut	*Bayrūt*	٣ - بيروت
Damascus	*Dimashq*	دمشق
Amman	*'ammān*	عمّان
Baghdad	*Baghdād*	بغداد
Tunis	*Tūnis*	تونس
Cairo	*Al-Qāhira*	القاهرة

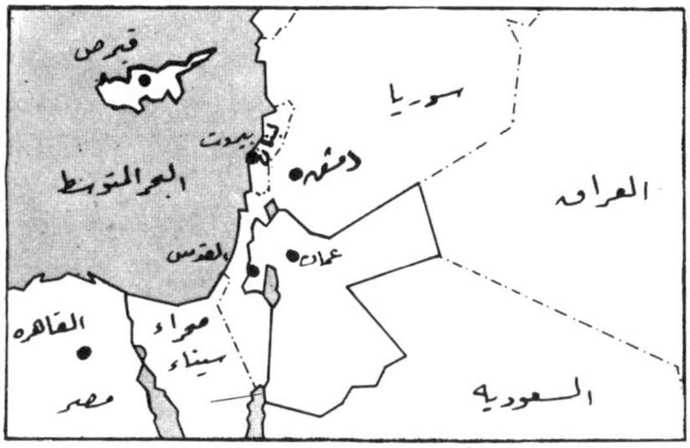

مع المدن العربية

دِمشق القديمة (لوحة للفنان ناظم الجعفري)

Riyadh	*Ar-Riyāḍ*	الرياض
Algiers	*Al-Jazā'ir*	الجزائر
Rabat	*Ar-Rabāṭ*	الرباط
Khartoum	*Al-Khartūm*	الخرطوم
Jerusalem	*Al-Quds*	القدس
Kuwait	*Al-Kuwayt* *(Al-Kuwait)*	الكويت

Kuwait (*Helmut Rehm*)

الكويت (هلموت ريم)

4-	What continent are you from? *(masc.,sing.)*	*Min ayyi qārratin anta?*	٤ ـ من أيّ قارّة أنتَ؟
	What continent are you from? *(fem.,sing.)*	*Min ayyi qārratin anti?*	من أيّ قارّة أنتِ؟
	I am from Asia	*Anā min Āsyā*	أنا من آسيا
	I am from Africa	*Anā min Ifrīqyā*	أنا من إفريقيا
		etc...	إلخ . . .
5-	What is your address? *(masc.,sing.)*	*Mā huwa ʻunwānuka?*	٥ ـ ما هو عنوانك؟
	What is your address? *(fem.,sing.)*	*Mā huwa ʻunwānuki?*	ما هو عنوانكِ؟
	My address...	*ʻunwānī...*	عنواني . . .
	Street...	*S͟hāriʻ...*	شارع . . .
	Number...	*Raqm...*	رقم . . .

نعم. أنا طالب

6-	Are you a student? *(masc.,sing.)*	*Hal anta ṭālibun?* *(or ṭālib)*	٦ ـ هل أنتَ طالب؟
	Yes. I am a student	*Naʻam. Anā ṭālibun* *(or ṭālib)*	نعم. أنا طالب.
	What are you studying? (masc., sing.)	*Māḏhā tadrusu?*	ماذا تدرس؟

	English	Transliteration	Arabic
	I am studying (I study) the Arabic language	*Adrusu‿l‿lughata‿l‿'arabiya*	أدرس اللغة العربية .
7-	Are you a student? *(fem.,sing.)*	*Hal anti ṭālibatun?* *(or ṭāliba)*	٧ ـ هل أنتِ طالبة؟
	Yes. I am a student	*Na'am. Anā ṭālibatun* *(or ṭāliba)*	نعم . أنا طالبة .
	What are you studying? *(fem.,sing.)*	*Mādhā tadrusīna?*	ماذا تدرسين؟
	I am studying the Arabic language	*Adrusu‿l‿lughata‿l‿'arabiya*	أدرس اللغة العربية .
8-	What do you study? (what are you studying? *masc.,sing.)*	*Mādhā tadrusu?*	٨ ـ ماذا تدرس؟
	What do you study? (What are you studying? *fem.,sing.)*	*Mādhā tadrusīna?*	ماذا تدرسين؟
	I study the English language	*Adrusu‿l‿lughata‿l‿ingliziya*	أدرس اللغة الإنكليزية .
	I study the French language	*Adrusu‿l-lughata‿l-faransiya*	أدرس اللغة الفرنسية .
	I study the Spanish language	*Adrusu‿l lughata‿l-ispāniya*	أدرس اللغة الإسبانية .
	I study the Russian language	*Adrusu‿l-lughata‿r-rūsiya*	أدرس اللغة الروسية
	I study the German language	*Adrusu‿l-lughata‿l-almāniya*	أدرس اللغة الألمانية .
	I study the Chinese language	*Adrusu‿l-lughata‿ṣ-ṣiniya*	أدرس اللغة الصينية .
	I study the Japanese language	*Adrusu‿l-lughata‿l-yābāniya*	أدرس اللغة اليابانية .
	I study the Hebrew language	*Adrusu‿l-lughata‿l-'ibriya*	أدرس اللغة العبرية .
	I study the Greek language	*Adrusu‿l-lughata‿l-yūnāniya*	أدرس اللغة اليونانية .

I study the Latin language	*Adrusu'l-lughata'l-lātīniya*	أدرس اللغة اللاتينية .
	etc...	إلخ . . .
9- I study Islamic history	*Adrusu't-tārīkha'l-islāmī*	٩ ـ أدرس التاريخ الإسلامي .
I study Greek history	*Adrusu't-tārīkha'l-yūnānī*	أدرس التاريخ اليوناني .
I study Russian history	*Adrusu't-tārīkha'r-rūsī*	أدرس التاريخ الروسي .
I study American history	*Adrusu't-tārīkha'l-amrīkī*	أدرس التاريخ الأمريكي .
	etc...	إلخ . . .
10- I study physics	*Adrusu'l-fīzyā'*	١٠ ـ أدرس الفيزياء .
I study chemistry	*Adrusu'l-kīmyā'*	أدرس الكيمياء .
I study geography	*Adrusu'l-jughrāfyā*	أدرس الجغرافيا .
I study philosophy	*Adrusu'l-falsafa*	أدرس الفلسفة .
I study algebra	*Adrusu'l-jabr*	أدرس الجبر.

2. FIVE CONNECTOR LETERS: ث ـ س ـ ش ـ ط ـ ظ

Name of the letter	Beginning of the word	Middle of the word	End of the word	Alone	Pronunciation
1. Thā'	ثـ	ـثـ	ـث	ث	same as thin

ثَريّ ـ ثابِت ـ روْث ـ رَوْث ـ وَثَبَ ـ بَثَّ

Name of the letter	Beginning of the word	Middle of the word	End of the word	Alone	Pronunciation
2. Sīn	سـ	ـسـ	ـس	س	same as sweet

سَبْت ـ سَراب ـ نَسَب ـ أَساس ـ أَساسي ـ سِوار

Name of the letter	Beginning of the word	Middle of the word	End of the word	Alone	Pronunciation
3. S̲hīn	شـ	ـشـ	ـش	ش	same as ship
4. Ṭā’	طـ	ـطـ	ـط	ط	no equivalent
5. Ẓā’	ظـ	ـظـ	ـظ	ظ	no equivalent

3. S̲hīn

شاي ـ شابّ ـ شَبابْ ـ شَيْب ـ بَشوشْ ـ بَشيْر

4. Ṭā’

طِبّ ـ طَبيْب ـ طاووس ـ بَطّ ـ بَطاطا ـ طينْ

5. Ẓā’

ظَنّ ـ أَظُنُّ ـ ظَهر ـ ظُهْر ـ نَظَرَ ـ ظَبي

3. Reading and Dictation

1. Dictation:

ثَوْب ـ ثَرْثار ـ ثَيِّب ـ سَيِّد ـ سادَ ـ سَدّ ـ سور ـ أَسْوَد ـ أَسَد ـ سُرور ـ سَريْر ـ شارِب ـ شاي ـ شَرّ ـ شاش ـ شَرِبَ ـ شَرِبَتْ ـ ريش ـ بَشير ـ شاويش ـ بَشوش ـ شُباط ـ رِباط ـ سَرَطان ـ سِراط .

2. Read and contrast:

تابَ ـ طابَ

توتْ ـ طوطْ

بَتَرْ ـ بَطَرْ

رَبَتَ ـ رَبَطَ

تينْ ـ طينْ

نَذَرَ ـ نَظَرَ

نَذير ـ نَظير

بَذَّ ـ بَظَّ

4. Review: *Letters and Words*

ثَري	wealthy
ثابِت	firm, stable
روث	Ruth
رَوْث	dung
وَثَبَ	he jumped
بَثَّ	he propagated
سَبْت	Saturday
سَراب	mirage
نَسَب	lineage, kinship
أَساس	foundation
أَساسي	fundamental, basic
سِوار	bracelet
شاي	tea
شابّ	young man
شَباب	youth
شَيْب	grayness
بَشوش	friendly, cheerful
بَشير	bringer of glad tidings, also a man's name
طِبّ	medicine
طَبيب	physician
طاووس	peacock
بَطّ	duck

بَطاطا	potato
طين	mud
ظَنّ	assumption, doubt
أَظُنُّ	I suppose, think
ظَهْر	back
ظُهْر	noon
نَظَرَ	he looked
ظَبي	gazelle
ثَوْب	dress
ثَرْثار	chatterbox, talkative
ثَيِّب	widow, divorcée
سَيِّد	Mister, Sir
سادَ	he became head, he ruled
سَدّ	dam, dike
سور	fence, wall
أَسْوَد	black
أَسَد	lion
سُرور	joy, happiness
سَرير	bed
شارِب	drinker
شَرّ	evil
شاش	gauze
شَرِبَ	he drank

شَرِبَتْ	she drank
ريشْ	feather
بَشيرْ	messenger, also a man's name
شاويشْ	a military rank, approx.: staff sergant
بَشوشْ	smiling, cheerful
شُباطْ	February
رِباط	ribbon, bond
سَرَطانْ	cancer
سِراطْ	way, path
تابَ	he repented
طابَ	something was delightful, delicious
توتْ	mulberry
طوطْ	the sound of an automobile horn
بَتَرَ	he cut off
بَطَرْ	wantonness, vanity
رَبَتَ	he patted
رَبَطَ	he tied up, fastened
تينْ	figs
طينْ	mud
نَذَرَ	he made a vow
نَظَرَ	he looked
نَذيرْ	warner, herald
نَظيرْ	equal, matching
بَذَّ	he surpassed
بَظَّ	he spouted

UNIT V

1. Conversation

		Transliteration	
1-	What do you study? (What are you studying? *masc.,sing.)*	*Mādhā tadrusu?*	١ ـ ماذا تدرس؟
	What do you study? (What are you studying? *fem.,sing.)*	*Mādhā tadrusīna?*	ماذا تدرسين؟
	I study Islamic art	*Adrusu‿l-fanna‿l-islāmī*	أدرس الفنّ الإسلامي .
	I study Greek art	*Adrusu‿l-fanna‿l-yūnānī*	أدرس الفنّ اليوناني .
	I study Byzantine art	*Adrusu‿l-fanna‿l-bīzanṭī*	أدرس الفنّ البيزنطي .
	I study European art	*Adrusu‿l-fanna‿l-awruppī*	أدرس الفنّ الأوربي .
	I study Japanese art	*Adrusu‿l-fanna‿l-yābānī* *etc...*	أدرس الفنّ الياباني . إلخ . . .
2-	I study medicine	*Adrusu‿ṭ-ṭibb*	٢ ـ أدرس الطبّ .
3-	I study linguistics	*Adrusu 'ilma‿l-lugha*	٣ ـ أدرس علم اللغة .
4-	I study sociology	*Adrusu 'ilma‿l-ijtimā'*	٤ ـ أدرس علم الاجتماع .
5-	I study law	*Adrusu‿l-ḥuqūq*	٥ ـ أدرس الحقوق .
6-	I study economics	*Adrusu‿l-iqtiṣād*	٦ ـ أدرس الاقتصاد .

I study Islamic Art أدرس الفن الإسلامي

Transliteration

7- I study Arabic literature	*Adrusu‿l-adaba‿l'arabī*	٧ ـ أدرس الأدب العربي .
I study English literature	*Adrusu‿l-adaba‿l-inglīzī*	أدرس الأدب الإنكليزي .
I study French literature	*Adrusu‿l-adaba‿l-faransī*	أدرس الأدب الفرنسي .
I study Spanish literature	*Adrusu‿l-adaba‿l-ispānī* *etc...*	أدرس الأدب الإسباني . إلخ . . .
8- Where do you live? *(masc.,sing.)*	*Ayna taskunu?*	٨ ـ أين تسكن؟
Where do you live? *(fem.,sing.)*	*Ayna taskunīna?*	أين تسكنين؟
I live in... street	*Askunu fī shāri'i...*	أسكن في شارع . . .
Number...	*Raqm...*	رقم . . .
I live in the city of...	*Askunu fī madīnati...*	أسكن في مدينة . . .

Transliteration

9- What is your telephone number? (masc., sing.)	*Mā huwa raqmu hātifika?*	٩ ـ ما هو رقم هاتفك؟
What is your telephone number? (fem., sing.)	*Mā huwa raqmu hātifiki?*	ما هو رقم هاتفكِ؟
My telephone number is...	*Raqmu hātifī...*	رقم هاتفي . . .

2. Five connector letters: م ـ ل ـ ك ـ ج ـ ح

1. Mīm

ـمـ   ـمـ   ـم   م   same as mother

مَنْظَر ـ باميا ـ سمر ـ ثوم ـ بوم ـ رُمّان ـ بَهيم ـ مَوْرِد ـ موز ـ موريتـانيا ـ مَطّاط

2. Lām

لـ   ـلـ   ـل   ل   same as lamb

Note: لا = لـ + ا

طالِبٌ ـ طَلَبَ ـ باطِـل ـ بَطَل ـ ظـالِم ـ ظُلْم ـ ظَلام ـ لا ـ بَلَد ـ بِـلاد ـ ظِلّ ـ ذُلّ ـ لَيْسَ سليمٌ طالباً

3. Kāf

كـ   ـكـ   ـك   ك   same as kind

كِتـابٌ ـ هذا كِتـابي ـ كَتَبَ ـ مَكْتوب ـ كَنَـدا ـ كوكـاكولا ـ بـانكـوك ـ شَكّ ـ شاكّ ـ مُبارَك ـ سمك

4. Jīm

جـ   ـجـ   ـج   ج   same as Jim

جَمَـلٌ ـ جَمـال ـ جَميـل ـ مَجْنـون ـ دَجـاج ـ زَوْج ـ ثَلْج ـ زَواج ـ جَـوْز ـ جَواز ـ أَنْتَجَ ـ بنجاب

5. Ḥā’

ـح ـحـ حـ ح no equivalent

حُبّ - حَبيْب - حَبيبي - حَبيْبَتي - حـارّ - بَحْر - مُبـاح - حَـرْب - حُلْم -
حَبُّ الشَّباب

3. Writing and reading:

1. Read and contrast:

هال - حال	فَهْم - فَحْم
هَوْل - حَوْل	توت - طوط
هَلَّ - حَلَّ	بَتَرَ - بَطَرَ
هَبَّ - حَبَّ	رَبَتَ - رَبَطَ
هاءْ - حاءْ	تِلالْ - طِلالْ
نَبَهَ - نَبَحَ	

4. Review: *letters and words*

Mauritania	موريتانيا	view, sight	مَنْظَر
rubber	مَطّاطْ	okra	باميا
student	طالِبْ	nightly chat, also a woman’s name	سَمَرْ
he ordered, re-quested	طَلَبَ	garlic	ثومْ
untrue, groundless	باطِلْ	owl	بومْ
hero	بَطَل	pomegranate	رُمّانْ
unjust	ظالِم	jet-black	بَهيمْ
injustice	ظُلْمْ	resource, source of income	مَوْرِدْ
darkness	ظَلام		
not, no	لا	banana	موزْ

بَلَدْ	country, town
بِلاد	country
ظِلّ	shadow
ذُلّ	shame, disgrace
لَيْسَ سَليم طالباً	Salim is not a student
كِتابْ	book
هذا كِتابي	this is my book
كَتَبَ	he wrote
مَكْتوبْ	written, letter
كَنَدا	Canada
كوكاكولا	cola
بانْكوكْ	Bangkok
شَكّ	doubt
شاكٌّ	skeptical
مُبارَكْ	blessed
سَمَكْ	fish
جَمَلْ	camel
جَمالْ	beauty
جَميلْ	beautiful
مَجْنونْ	crazy
دَجاج	chickens
زَوْج	husband
ثَلْج	snow
زَواج	marriage
جَوْزْ	walnut
جَوازْ	passport
أَنْتَجَ	he produced
بنجابْ	Punjab
حُبّ	love
حَبيبْ	lover
حَبيبي	my love, masc.
حَبيبَتي	my love, fem.
حارّ	hot
بَحْر	sea
مُباحْ	permitted, legal
حَرْبْ	war
حُلْم	dream
حَبُّ الشباب	pimples
هالْ	cardamon
حالْ	condition, state
هَوْلْ	terror, fright
حَوْلْ	year, power
هَلَّ	he appeared
حَلَّ	he solved, deciphered
هَبَّ	he got in motion, proceeded abruptly
حَبَّ	he loved
هاءْ	name of the letter هـ
حاءْ	name of the letter ح

نَبَه	he became well-known
نَبَحَ	It barked
فَهْم	understanding
فَحْم	coal
توت	mulberry
طوط	the sound of an automobile horn
بَتَرَ	he cut off
بَطِرَ	he was wanton, vain
رَبَتَ	he patted
رَبَطَ	he tied up
تِلال	hills
طِلال	dew, drizzle

UNIT VI

1. Conversation

		Transliteration	
1-	What do you study? (What are you studying? *masc.,sing.)*	*Mādhā tadrusu?*	١ ـ ماذا تدرس؟
	What do you study? (What are you studying? *fem.,sing.)*	*Mādhā tadrusīna?*	ماذا تدرسين؟
	I study commerce	*Adrusu‿t-tijāra*	أدرس التجارة .
	I study political sciences	*Adrusu‿l'ulūma‿s-siyāsiya*	٢ ـ أدرس العلوم السياسية .
	I study sciences	*Adrusu‿l'ulūm*	٣ ـ أدرس العلوم .
	I study psychology	*Adrusu 'ilma‿n-nafs*	٤ ـ أدرس علم النّفس .
5	Where do you live? *(masc.,sing.)*	*Ayna taskunu?*	٥ ـ أين تسكن؟
	Where do you live? *(fem.,sing.)*	*Ayna taskunīna?*	أين تسكنين؟
	I live in... street	*Askunu fī shāri'i...*	أسكن في شارع . . .
	Number...	*Raqm...*	رقم . . .
	Do you live alone? *(masc.,sing.)*	*Hal taskunu waḥdaka?*	هل تسكن وحدكَ؟

Transliteration

	English	Transliteration	Arabic
	Do you live alone? *(fem.,sing.)*	*Hal taskunīna waḥdaki?*	هل تسكنين وحدكِ؟
	Yes. I live alone	*Na'am. Askunu waḥdī*	نعم . أسكن وحدي .
6-	Do you live alone? *(masc.,sing.)*	*Hal taskunu waḥdaka?*	٦ ـ هل تسكن وحدكَ؟
	Do you live alone? *(fem.,sing.)*	*Hal taskunīna waḥdaki?*	هل تسكنين وحدكِ؟
	No. I live with my girl-friend	*Lā. Askunu ma'a ṣadīqatī*	لا . أسكن مع صديقتي .
	No. I live with my boyfriend	*Lā. Askunu ma'a ṣadīqī*	لا . أسكن مع صديقي .

أُسرة قروية فلسطينية
(للفنان أحمد أبو حجاب)

	English	Transliteration	Arabic
7-	No. I live with my parents	*Lā. Askunu ma'a wālidayy*	٧ ـ لا . أسكن مع والديّ .
8-	No. I live with my wife	*Lā. Askunu ma'a zawjatī*	٨ ـ لا . أسكن مع زوجتي .
	No. I live with my hus-band	*Lā. Askunu ma'a zawjī*	لا . أسكن مع زوجي .

	Transliteration	
9- Where were you born? *(masc.,sing.)*	*Ayna wulidta?*	٩ - أين وُلدتَ؟
Where were you born? *(fem.,sing.)*	*Ayna wulidti?*	أين وُلدتِ؟
I was born in the city of...	*Wulidtu fī madīnati...*	ولدت في مدينة . . .
10- What is your profession? *(masc.,sing.)*	*Mā hiya mihnatuka?*	١٠ -ما هي مهنتكَ؟
What is your profession? *(fem.,sing.)*	*Mā hiya mihnatuki?*	ما هي مهنتكِ؟
I am a student *(masc.)*	*Anā ṭālibun* (or *ṭālib*)	أنا طالب .
I am a student *(fem.)*	*Anā ṭālibatun* (or *ṭāliba*)	أنا طالبة .
I am a professor *(masc.)*	*Anā ustā<u>dh</u>un* (or *ustā<u>dh</u>*)	أنا أستاذ .
I am a professor *(fem.)*	*Anā ustā<u>dh</u>atun* (or *ustā<u>dh</u>a*)	أنا أستاذة .
I am a doctor *(masc.)*	*Anā ṭabībun* (or *ṭabīb*)	أنا طبيب .
I am a doctor *(fem.)*	*Anā ṭabībatun* (or *ṭabība*)	أنا طبيبة .

2. Five connector letters: خ - ف - ق - ص - ض

1. <u>Kh</u>ā'

خ ـخ ـخـ خـ — no equivalent, same as German Bach

خَدّ - خَيْر - خَبَر - أَخْبار - شَخَرَ - شَيْخ - تاريخ - باخَ - خُرْطوم

2. Fā'

ف ـف ـفـ فـ same as father

فَنّ ـ فَنّان ـ ظَريف ـ سَيْف ـ فُرْن ـ سافَرَ ـ خَروف ـ خافَ

3. Qāf

ق ـق ـقـ قـ no equivalent

قارِب ـ قَبَّلَ ـ قَبْل الظهـر ـ تَقَدَّمَ بِـطَلَب ـ بَقْ بَقْ بَقْ ـ دِمَشْق ـ شَرْق ـ
الشَّرْقُ الأوْسَط ـ مُسْتَشْرِق ـ قُرْآن ـ قَرَأَ ـ بَقَر ـ قَبْقاب

4. Ṣād

ص ـص ـصـ صـ no equivalent

صُرْصـور ـ صَباحَ الخَـيْر ـ لِصّ ـ صَيّـاد ـ صـوص ـ صَفّ ـ صُنْـدوق
البَريْد ـ صَيْف ـ صابون ـ صُبّيْر ـ صَبْر

5. Ḍād

ض ـض ـضـ ضـ no equivalent

ضَرَبَ ـ واضِح ـ هَلْ هَذا واضِح ؟ ـ مَريْض ـ أَبْيَض ـ البَحْر الأَبْيَض ـ
أَرْض ـ بَيْض

3. Writing and reading

1. Read and contrast:

كَلْبٌ ـ قَلْبٌ
كَبَّلَ ـ قَبَّلَ
شَرِكَ ـ شَرِقَ

سوس ـ صوص
سادَ ـ صادَ
سارَ ـ صارَ
سيْنْ ـ صيْنْ
سَبَرَ ـ صَبَرَ

دَرْب ـ ضَرْب

دارْ ـ ضارّ

دَلَّ ـ ضَلَّ

دالْ ـ ضالْ

دِرْع ـ ضَرْع

دَرَّسَ ـ ضَرَّسَ

دَهْر ـ ضَهْر

ذَرْف ـ ظَرْف

ذُلّ ـ ظِلّ

رَجُلٌ فَذٌّ بَذٌّ ـ رَجُلٌ فَظٌّ بَظٌّ

4. Review: *Letters and Words*

خَدّ	cheek
خَيْرْ	good thing, welfare
خَبَرْ	one item of the news
أَخْبارْ	news
شَخَرَ	he snored
شَيْخ	an elderly
تاريخ	history
باخَ	he faded
خُرْطومْ	trunk (of the elephant)
فَنّ	art
فَنّانْ	artist
ظَريفْ	charming
سَيْفْ	sword
فُرْنْ	oven
سافَرَ	he went on a journey
خَروف	young sheep
خافَ	he was afraid

قارِب	boat
قَبَّلَ	he kissed
قَبْلَ الظهر	before noon, a.m.
تَقَدَّمَ بِطَلَب	he put in an application, (submitted....)
بَقْ بَقْ بَقْ	the sound of boiling water, also the sound of watar bubbles
دِمَشْق	Damascus
شَرْق	east
الشَّرْقُ الأَوْسَط	The Middle East
مُسْتَشْرِق	orientalist
قُرْآن	Koran
قَرَأَ	he read
بَقَر	cows
قَبْقاب	wooden clog
صُرْصور	cockroach
صَباح الخَيْر	good morning

لِصّ	thief
صَيّاد	fisherman
صوص	chick
صَفّ	class
صُنْدوقُ البَريد	post-office box
صَيْف	summer
صابون	soap
صُبَّيْر	Indian fig
صَبْر	patience, endurance
ضَرَبَ	he struck
واضِح	clear
هَلْ هَذا واضِح ؟	is this clear?
مَريْض	sick
أَبْيَض	white
البَحْرُ الأبْيَضُ المُتَوَسِّط	The Mediterranean Sea
أَرْضْ	earth, land
بَيْضْ	eggs
كَلْب	dog
قَلْب	heart
كَبَّلَ	he put in irons
قَبَّلَ	he kissed
شَرِكَ	he shared
شَرِقَ	he swallowed the wrong way
سوس	woodworm

صوص	chick
سادَ	he became chief, he ruled
صادَ	he caught (a fish), he hunted (a game)
سارَ	he moved on, walked
صارَ	he became
سينْ	name of the letter س
صينْ (الصين)	China
سَبَرَ	he examined with a probe
صَبَرَ	he was patient
دَرْبْ	path, track, alley
ضَرْبْ	beating
دارْ	house
ضارّ	harmful
دَلَّ	he pointed at
ضَلَّ	he lost his way
دالْ	name of the letter د
ضالٌّ	astray, lost
دِرْع	coat of mail
ضَرْع	udder
دَرَّسَ	he taught
ضَرَّسَ	it rendered dull (the teeth by acid food and drink - colloquial)
دَهْر	age, epoch, lifetime

ضَهْر	top, summit	ظِلّ	shadow
ذَرْف	shedding (tears)	رَجُلٌ فَذٌّ بَذٌّ	an exceptional man
ظَرْف	envelope	رَجُلٌ فَظٌّ بَظٌّ	a rude gross man
ذُلّ	shame, disgrace		

UNIT VII

1. Conversation

	Transliteration	
1- Are you married? *(masc.,sing.)*	*Hal anta mutazawijun? (or mutazawij)*	١ ـ هل أنتَ متزوِّج؟
Yes. I am married *(masc.)*	*Na'am anā mutazawijun (or mutazawij)*	نعم. أنا متزوِّج.
2- Are you married? *(fem.,sing.)*	*Hal anti mutazawijatun? (or mutazawija)*	٢ ـ هل أنتِ متزوِّجة؟
Yes. I am married *(fem.)*	*Na'am anā mutazawijatun (or mutazawija)*	نعم. أنا متزوِّجة.
3- No. I am single *(masc.)*	*Lā. Anā a'zab*	٣ ـ لا. أنا أعزب.
No. I am single *(fem.)*	*Lā. Anā 'azbā'*	لا. أنا عزباء.
4- How many children have you got? *(masc., sing.)*	*Kam waladan ladayka?*	٤ ـ كم ولداً لديكَ؟
How many children have you got? *(fem , sing.)*	*Kam waladan ladayki?*	كم ولداً لديكِ؟
I have one child	*Ladayya waladun wāḥid*	لديّ ولد واحد.
I have two children	*Ladayya waladān*	لديّ ولدان.

Transliteration

	Transliteration	
I have three children	*Ladayya thalāthatu awlād*	لديّ ثلاثة أولاد .
I have four children	*Ladayya arbaʻatu awlād*	لديّ أربعة أولاد .
I have no children	*Laysa ladayya awlād*	ليس لديّ أولاد .
5- How old are you? *(masc.,sing.)*	*Kam ʻumruka?*	٥ ـ كم عمركَ؟
How old are you? *(fem.,sing.)*	*Kam ʻumruki?*	كم عمركِ؟
6. I am twenty years old	*ʻumrī ʻishrūna sana*	٦ ـ عمري عشرون سنة .
I am thirty years old	*ʻumrī thalāthūna sana*	عمري ثلاثون سنة .
I am forty years old	*ʻumrī arbaʻūna sana*	عمري أربعون سنة .
I am fifty years old	*ʻumrī khamsūna sana*	عمري خمسون سنة .
I am sixty years old	*ʻumrī sittūna sana*	عمري ستّون سنة .
I am seventy years old	*ʻumrī sabʻūna sana*	عمري سبعون سنة .
I am eighty years old	*ʻumrī thamānūna sana*	عمري ثمانون سنة .
I am ninety years old	*ʻumrī tisʻūna sana*	عمري تسعون سنة .
I am one hundred years old	*ʻumrī mi'atu sana*	عمري مئة سنة .

2. Two connector letters:

ع - غ

1. ʻayn

no equivalent	ع	ـع	ـعـ	عـ

عـامِل ـ عُـمّال ـ حِزْبُ العُـمّال ـ بَعْـدَ الـظُّهْـر ـ صَعْب ـ مُجْتَمَـع ـ عِلْمُ الاجْتِماع ـ مَوْضوع ـ سَمِعَ ـ عَمّ ـ عِنَب ـ شَعْـر ـ مَـعَ ـ عـالِم ـ عُنْف ـ التَّمْييزُ العُنْصُري ـ إصْبَع

2. Ghayn

غ ـغ ـغـ غـ no equivalent

غداً - غِلاف - شـاغِر - بَغْـداد - مُغَنّي - غَرْب - غَـداء - بالِـغ - بَلاغ - دِماغ

1. READ AND CONTRAST:

أَنْ - عَنْ   باءْ - باعْ

أَوْ - عَوْ   ماءْ - ماعْ

أَمْ - عَمْ   بَدَأَ - بَدَعَ

سَأَلَ - سَعَلَ   نَبَأْ - نَبْع

وَأَدَ - وَعَدَ

3. THE SUN AND THE MOON LETTERS

The letters ت - ث - د - ذ - ر - ز - س - ش - ص - ض - ط - ظ - ل -and ن are known as 'sun letters' in contrast to the 'moon letters' which constitute the rest of the alphabet. When a noun or an adjective defined by الـ (the) begins with one of the 'sun letters' the 'l' of the definite article is assimilated in pronunciation to the 'sun letter' which is written with *shadda*, e.g. الـرّابـع pronounced as ar-rābi', the fourth; الـدّرس pronounced as ad-dars, the lesson. Note however, that orientalists prefer to write the 'l' in transliteration although it has lost its sound in pronunciation.

1. WRITE THEN READ:

التّاريخ - الثّالث - الدَّرْس - الذَّكَر - الرّابع - الزّائر - السّابع - السَّيّارة - الشَّمْس - الصّورة - الضَّمير - الطّالب - الظَّرْف - النَّمِر - اللَّوْن.

4. THE TIED T التاء المربوطة

Note: The tied t (ة، ـة) which indicates the feminine gender in the nouns or adjectives occurs only as the last consonant of a word, e.g., مديرة، فتاة، أستاذة، طالبة

If a suffix however, is added to the word, the ة، ـة is changed to ت, e.g., مـديـرتي، فتاتي، أستاذتي، طالبتي

It is important to note that the 'alif which is normally written with the accusative nunation of a masculine noun, is not written after ـة ،ة e.g.,

طالباً a male student, but

طالبةً a female student.

The full form of the ـة ،ة in pronunciation is (atun or atan, or atin, e.g. طالبةٍ، طالبةً، طالبةٌ), while the pausal form is (a) in all cases and mostly at the end of sentences or complete clauses; e.g., ملكة, 'malika'. Thus, the tied t could be pronounced as 't' or 'a' according to its position in the sentence.

5. Writing and reading

1. Write then read:

طالبة - أستاذة - آنسة - سكرتيرة - مديرة - سيّدة - ملكة - مكتبة -
جامعة - سيّارة - طائرة - طبيبة - مراسلة - ساعة - طاولة - مجلّة -
غسّالة - لغة - الشيوعيّة - الاشتراكيّة - الرأسمالية

2. Put into the feminine, then read:

١ - أنا طالب.

أنا ــــــ.

٢ - هو أستاذ.

هي ــــــ.

٣ - أنتَ طبيب.

أنتِ ــــــ.

٤ - أنا مراسِل.

أنا ــــــ.

٥ - هو سكرتير.

هي ــــــ.

6. Alif maqsūra ى

In a number of Arabic words, a final long vowel aa is represented not by the usual'alif ا but by a special letter ى called ألف مقصورة or shortened 'alif, e.g., على، إلى، موسى، ليلى، مقهى، رمى، اشترى، نادى، رأى، بنى If a suffix is added, however, to such a word, the ى is often changed to ا, e.g., he called him, ناداه; he built it بناه; he saw him رآه, etc.

7. Review: *Letters and Words*

عامِلْ	worker
عُمّالْ	workers
حِزبُ العُمّال	the labor party
بَعْدَ الظُهْر	afternoon, p.m.
صَعْب	difficult
مُجْتَمَعْ	society
عِلْمُ الاِجْتِماعْ	sociology
مَوْضوعْ	topic, subject
سَمِعَ	he heard
عَمّ	uncle
عِنَبْ	grapes
شَعْر	hair
مَعَ	with
عالِم	scholar, scientist
عُنْف	violence
التَمْييزُ العنصري	racial discrimination
إصْبَعْ	finger
غداً	tomorrow
غِلاف	cover, jacket of a book
شاغِرْ	vacant
بَغْداد	Baghdad
مُغَنّي	singer
غَرْبْ	west
غَداءْ	lunch
بالِغْ	of age, mature
بَلاغْ	proclamation
دِماغْ	brain
أنْ	(conj) that
عَنْ	(prep) about
أَوْ	or
عَوْ	the sound of a barking dog
أَمْ	or? (introducing the second member of an alternative question)
عَمّْ	uncle
سَأَلَ	he asked
سَعَلَ	he coughed
وَأَدَ	he buried
وَعَدَ	he promised
باءْ	name of the letter ب
باعْ	he sold
ماءْ	water
ماعْ	he melted, dissolved
بَدَأَ	he began
بَدَعَ	he introduced, originated
نَبَأ	news item
نَبْعْ	spring, source
التّاريخ	the history
الثّالث	the third

الدَّرْس	the lesson
الذَّكَر	the male
الرّابِع	the fourth
الزّائِر	the visitor
السابِع	the seventh
السَّيّارة	the car
الشَّمْس	the sun
الصّورَة	the picture
الضَّمير	the conscience
الطالِب	the student
الظَّرف	the envelope
النَّمِر	the tiger
اللَّوْن	the color
طالِبَة	student, fem.
أُسْتاذة	professor, fem.
آنِسَة	young lady
سِكْرتيرَة	secretary, fem.
مُديرَة	director, fem.
سَيِّدَة	Mrs., lady
مَلَكَة	queen
مَكْتَبَة	library
جامِعَة	university
سَيّارَة	car
طائِرَة	airplane
طَبيبَة	physician, fem.
مُراسِلَة	correspondent, fem.
ساعة	watch, hour
طاوِلَة	table
مَجَلَّة	magazine
غَسّالَة	washerwoman, washing machine
لُغَة	language
الشيوعِيَّة	(the) communism
الاِشْتِراكِيَّة	(the) socialism
الرَّأْسمالِيَّة	(the) capitalism
نادى	he called
رَأى	he saw
بَنى	he built
عَلى	(prep.) on, upon
إِلى	(prep.) to, toward
موسى	Moses
لَيْلى	Layla: a woman's name
مَقْهى	café
رَمى	he threw
اِشْتَرى	he bought
ناداهُ	he called him
بَناهُ	he built it
رَآهُ	he saw him

UNIT VIII

1. Conversation

	Transliteration	
1- What is his name? *(masc.,sing.)*	*Ma‿smuhu?*	١ ـ ما اسمه؟
His name is…	*Ismuhu…*	اسمه . . .
What is her name? *(fem.,sing.)*	*Ma‿smuhā?*	ما اسمها؟
Her name is…	*Ismuhā…*	اسمها . . .
2- Where is he from?	*Min ayna huwa?*	٢ ـ من أين هو؟
He is from…	*Huwa min…*	هو من . . .
Where is she from?	*Min ayna hiya?*	من أين هي ؟
She is from…	*Hiya min…*	هي من . . .
3- How is he?	*Kayfa ḥāluhu?*	٣ ـ كيف حاله؟
Well	*Bik̲hayr*	بخير
How is she?	*Kayfa ḥāluhā?*	كيف حالها؟
Well	*Bik̲hayr*	بخير
4- Is he a student?	*Hal huwa ṭālibun? (or ṭālib)*	٤ ـ هل هو طالب؟

Transliteration

Yes. He is a student	*Na'am. Huwa ṭālibun*	نعم. هو طالب.
Is she a student?	*Hal hiya tālibatun?* (*or ṭāliba*)	هل هي طالبة؟
Yes. She is a student	*Na'am. Hiya ṭālibatun*	نعم. هي طالبة.
5- Is he a teacher?	*Hal huwa ustādhun?* (*or ustādh*)	٥ ـ هل هو أستاذ؟

من أين هو؟ هو طالب ألماني.

هل هي أستاذة؟

No. He is a student	*Lā. Huwa ṭālibun*	لا. هو طالب.
Is she a teacher?	*Ḥal hiya ustādhatun?* (*or ustādha*)	هل هي أستاذة؟
No. She is a student	*Lā. Hiya ṭālibatun*	لا. هي طالبة.
6- What country is he from?	*Min ayyi baladin huwa?*	٦ ـ من أيّ بلد هو؟
He is from...	*Huwa min...*	هو من...
What country is she from?	*Min ayyi baladin hiya?*	من أيّ بلد هي؟
She is from...	*Hiya min...*	هي من...
7- From which city is he?	*Min ayyi madīnatin huwa?*	٧ ـ من أيّ مدينة هو؟

Transliteration

	English	Transliteration	Arabic
	He is from the city of...	*Huwa min madīnati...*	هو من مدينة . . .
	From which city is she?	*Min ayyi madīnatin hiya?*	من أيّ مدينة هي ؟
	She is from the city of...	*Hiya min madīnati...*	هي من مدينة . . .
8-	What is his address?	*Mā huwa ʻunwānuhu?*	٨ ـ ما هو عنوانه؟
	His address is...	*ʻunwānuhu...*	عنوانه . . .
	What is her address?	*Mā huwa ʻunwānuhā?*	ما هو عنوانها؟
	Her address is...	*ʻunwānuhā...*	عنوانها . . .
9-	Is he married?	*Hal huwa mutazawijun?* *(or mutazawij)*	٩ ـ هل هو متزوِّج؟
	Yes. He is married	*Naʻam. Huwa mutazawijun*	نعم . هو متزوِّج .
	Is she married?	*Hal hiya mutazawijatun?* *(or mutazawija)*	هل هي متزوِّجة؟
	Yes. She is married	*Naʻam. Hiya mutazawijatun*	نعم . هي متزوِّجة .
10-	Eleven	*Aḥada ʻashar*	١٠ ـ أحد عشر ١١
	Twelve	*Ithnā ʻashar*	اثنا عشر ١٢
	Thirteen	*Thalāthata ʻashar*	ثلاثة عشر ١٣
	Fourteen	*Arbaʻata ʻashar*	أربعة عشر ١٤
	Fifteen	*Khamsata ʻashar*	خمسة عشر ١٥
	Sixteen	*Sittata ʻashar*	ستة عشر ١٦
	Seventeen	*Sabʻata ʻashar*	سبعة عشر ١٧
	Eighteen	*Thamāniyata ʻashar*	ثمانية عشر ١٨
	Nineteen	*Tisʻata ʻashar*	تسعة عشر ١٩
	Twenty	*ʻishrūn*	عشرون ٢٠

2. The definite article

1. The definite article for all cases, numbers and genders is . It is written prefixed to the defined noun or adjective, e.g.

The big house, *masc.,nom.case*	١ ـ البَيْتُ الكَبِيرُ
The big house, *masc.,acc.case*	البَيْتَ الكَبِيرَ
The big house, *masc.,gen.case*	البَيْتِ الكَبِيرِ
The teacher, *masc.*	٢ ـ المُدَرِّسُ
The teacher, *fem.*	المُدَرِّسَةُ
The teachers, *masc.*	٣ ـ المُدَرِّسونَ
The teachers, *fem.*	المُدَرِّساتُ

Note that the defined noun or adjective loses its nunation.

3. Reading and writing

(a)	1.	This is a big house	١ ـ هذا بَيْتٌ كَبِيرٌ
		This is the big house	هذا هُوَ البَيْتُ الكَبِيرُ
	2.	I saw a big house	٢ ـ رَأَيْتُ بَيْتاً كَبِيراً
		I saw the big house	رَأَيْتُ البَيْتَ الكَبِيرَ
	3.	I met (with) a housewife	٣ ـ اجْتَمَعْتُ بِرَبَّةِ بَيْتٍ
		I met (with) the housewife	اجْتَمَعْتُ بِرَبَّةِ البَيْتِ

Note: In all these examples, the word 'house', whether it is the subject, object or in the genitive case, defined, or undefined, remains unchanged in English. The same applies to the adjective 'big'. But this is not the case in Arabic.

nom. indefinite	*hā<u>dh</u>ā baytun kabīrun*	this is a big house
nom. definite	*hā<u>dh</u>ā huwa-l-baytu-l kabīru*	this is the big house

acc. indefinite	*ra'aytu baytan kabīran*	I saw a big house
acc, definite	*ra'aytu‿l bayta‿l kabīra*	I saw the big house
gen. indefinite	*ijtama'tu birabbati baytin*	I met (with) a housewife
gen. definite	*ijtama'tu birabbati‿l bayti*	I met (with) the housewife

(b)	1.	This is an English student	١ - هَذا طالِبٌ إنْكليْزِيٌّ
		This is the English student	هَذا هُوَ الطّالِبُ الإنْكليزيُّ
	2.	I saw an English student	٢ - رَأَيْتُ طالِباً إنْكليزيّاً
		I saw the English student	رَأَيْتُ الطّالِبَ الإنْكليزيَّ
	3.	This is a house of an English student	٣ - هَذا هُوَ بَيْتُ طالِبٍ إنْكليزيٍّ
		This is the house of the English student	هَذا هُوَ بَيْتُ الطّالِبِ الإنْكليزيِّ
(c)	1.	This is a book	١ - هَذا كِتابٌ
		This is the book	هَذا هُوَ الكِتابُ
	2.	I read a book	٢ - قَرَأْتُ كِتاباً
		I read the book	قَرَأْتُ الكِتابَ
	3.	This is a cover of a book	٣ - هذا هُوَ غِلافُ كتابٍ
		This is the cover of the book	هذا هُوَ غِلافُ الكِتابِ
(d)	1.	This is an Arab student *fem.*	١ - هَذِهِ طالِبَةٌ عَرَبِيَّةٌ
		This is the Arab student *fem.*	هَذِهِ هِيَ الطّالِبَةُ العَرَبِيَّةُ
	2.	I saw an Arab student *fem.*	٢ - رَأَيْتُ طالِبَةً عَرَبِيَّةً
		I saw the Arab student *fem.*	رَأَيْتُ الطّالِبَةَ العَرَبِيَّةَ

3.	I met (with) an Arab student *fem.*	٣ ـ اجْتَمَعْتُ بِطالِبَةٍ عَرَبِيَّةٍ
	I met (with) the Arab student *fem.*	اجْتَمَعْتُ بالطّالِبَةِ العَرَبِيَّةِ

Reading

1. Put in the definite article and read aloud:

١ ـ هذا هو طالبٌ لبنانيٌّ .

٢ ـ رأيت طالباً لبنانيّاً .

٣ ـ اجتمعتُ بطالبٍ لبنانيٍّ .

١ ـ هذه هي طالبةٌ فَرَنْسِيَّةٌ .

٢ ـ رأيت طالبةً فَرَنْسِيَّةً .

٣ ـ اجتمعت بطالبةٍ فَرَنْسِيَّةٍ .

2. Change the underlined nouns and adjectives into indefinite expressions and read aloud:

١ ـ هذا هو البيتُ الكبيرُ .

٢ ـ رأيت البيتَ الكبيرَ .

٣ ـ هذه هي ربّةُ البيتِ .

١ ـ هذه هي الطبيبةُ المِصْريَّةُ .

٢ ـ رأيت الطبيبةَ المِصْريَّةَ .

٣ ـ اجتمعت بالطبيبةِ المِصْريَّةِ .

١ ـ هذا هو المدرّسُ العربيُّ .

٢ ـ رأيت المدرّسَ العربيَّ .

٣ ـ اجتمعت بالمدرّسِ العربيِّ في المكتبة .

3. Note that the definite article الـ is used before some Arabic cities and countries:

١ ـ القدس　　　　٢ ـ القاهرة

٣ ـ الإسكندرية

٤ ـ الرياض

٥ ـ الجزائر

٦ ـ الخرطوم

٧ ـ البصرة

٨ ـ الرباط

٩ ـ الدار البيضاء

مدينة الجزائر

١ ـ الأردن

٢ ـ الإمارات العربية المتحدة

٣ ـ الكويت

٤ ـ البحرين

٥ ـ الجزائر

٦ ـ المملكة العربية السعودية

٧ ـ السودان

٨ ـ الصومال

٩ ـ العراق

١٠ ـ المغرب

١١ ـ اليمن

UNIT IX

1. Conversation

The teacher will help the students memorize the first six sentences of Lesson 1: *At The Airport* without referring to the printed text. The dialogue takes place between two males.

		Transliteration	
1-	At the airport	*Fīl maṭār*	١ ـ في المطار
2-	John: What a surprise!	*Yālalmufāja'ati!*	٢ ـ جون : يا للمفاجأة !
	What are you doing here?	*Mādhā taf'alu hunā?*	ماذا تفعل هنا؟
3-	Peter: I was on a short visit to Beirut. And You?	*Kuntu fī ziyāratin qaṣīratin libayrūt. Wa anta?*	٣ ـ بيتر: كنتُ في زيارة قصيرة لبيروت . وأنتَ؟
4-	John: I want to study Arabic	*Urīdu an adrusal 'arabiya*	٤ ـ جون : أريد أن أدرس العربية .
5-	Peter: Really? Are you crazy?	*Ḥaqqan? hal anta majnūn?*	٥ ـ بيتر: حقاً ؟ هل أنت مجنون؟
6-	John: Perhaps	*Rubbamā*	٦ ـ جون : ربما .

UNIT X

1. Conversation

The teacher will help the students memorize the rest of Lesson 1: *At The Airport* without referring to the printed text. The dialogue takes place between two males.

	Transliteration	
1- Peter: O.K.	*Ḥasanan.*	١ ـ بيتر: حسناً.
I'm in a hurry	*Anā 'alā 'ajala*	أنا على عجلة.
2- Write to me to my address in London	*Uktub lī ilā 'unwānī fī landon*	٢ ـ أُكتب لي إلى عنواني في لندن.
3- Do you promise me that?	*Hal ta'idunī bidhālik?*	٣ ـ هل تعدني بذلك؟
4- John: Yes, Yes	*Na'am. Na'am*	٤ ـ جون: نعم. نعم.
5- Peter: So long	*Ilal-liqā'*	٥ ـ بيتر: إلى اللقاء.
6- John: So long	*Ilal-liqā'*	٦ ـ جون: إلى اللقاء.

UNIT XI

1. Conversation

Review Lesson 1: *At The Airport* without referring to the printed text. Each student whether male, or female ought to be able to play the role of either John or Peter. Once the dialogue is mastered slight changes to the text will be gradually allowed.

Transliteration

1- What are you doing here? *(fem.,sing.)*	*Mādhā taf'alīna hunā?*	١ ـ ماذا تفعلين هنا؟
2- And you? *(fem.,sing.)*	*Wa anti?*	٢ ـ وأنتِ؟
3- Are you crazy? *(fem.,sing.)*	*Hal anti majnūna?*	٣ ـ هل أنتِ مجنونة؟
4- Write to me *(fem.,sing.)*	*Uktubī lī*	٤ ـ أُكتبي لي .
Do you promise me that? *(fem.,sing.)*	*Hal ta'idīnanī bidhālik?*	٥ ـ هل تعدينني بذلك؟

2. Hamzat-al-waṣl

Hamzat-al-waṣl, or "the joining hamza" always occurs at the beginning of a word. Its vowel is written above or below 'alif, e.g.,

إِذْهَبْ، أُكْتُبْ، إِمْرَأَةٌ، إِسْمي، إِبْنَتي، إِبْني، إِثْنان، اَلمكتب، إِسْتَخْرَجَ، إِنْتَهى، إِنْفِجار.

If any other word, however, precedes these words hamzat-al-waṣl and its vowel must be omitted. The sign of the omission is ص and is found in the *Quran* and some printed books, e.g.,

باب ٱلمكتب، ما ٱسمك؟ هذا ٱبنه، قال: ٱمرأتي مريضة.

1. READ OUT LOUD AND COMPARE BETWEEN THE FOLLOWING WORDS:

What is your name?	ما ٱسْمُكَ؟	My name	اِسْمي
Where is your son?	أَيْنَ ٱبْنُكَ؟	My son	اِبْني
Is this your wife?	هَلْ هَذِهِ ٱمْرَأَتُكَ؟	My wife	اِمْرَأَتي
What is the name of your daughter?	ما ٱسْمُ ٱبْنَتِكَ؟	My daughter	اِبْنَتي
After electing him for the presidency…	بَعْدَ ٱنْتِخابِهِ للرئاسَةِ	Election	اِنْتِخاب
Write and read!	أُكْتُبْ وٱقْرَأْ	Read!	اِقْرَأْ

3. HAMZA: *AT THE BEGINNING, MIDDLE, OR END OF THE WORD.*

1. At the beginning of a word *hamza* is always written on ‘alif e.g., أكل (’akala: he ate), أنا (’anā: I am), أنت (’anta: you are), أستاذ (’ustādh: a teacher), إنسان (’insān: a human being).

2. In the middle or at the end of a word, *hamza* is written on ا، و or ى (without the dots) or standing alone on the line according to the vowels that come before and after, e.g.

1. سَأَلَ sa’ala: he asked.

Other examples: قَرَأَ، بَدَأَ، ثَأْر، فَجْأة

2. سُئِلَ su’ila: he was asked.

Other examples: يَئِسَ

3. جَرُؤَ jaru’a: he was bold.

Other examples: يُؤَدي ، مُؤْمِن

Note: The student should always bear in mind that the 'i' sound is the strongest, then follows the 'u' sound, and lastly, the 'a' sound. Therefore, the 'i' sound always wins if competing with an 'u' or 'a' sound, and the *hamza* is then written on an ى seat. The 'u' sound is also stronger than the 'a' sound, consequently, the *hamza* will be written on و seat, and so forth.

4. (a) *Hamza* stands alone on the line at the end of a word when it follows a consonant or long vowel, e.g.

جُزْء، ضَوْء، بَدْء، ماء، سوء، مَساء، جاء، وُضوء، مُروءَة، حَياء

(b) Hamza stands alone on the line in the middle of a word after و ,

e.g., مروءات، تـوءمـان or between two 'alifs إحصاءات، إجراءات

3. Nunation after hamza:

If an indefinite masculine word ends with *hamza* on or after an 'alif and happens to be in the accusative case, it does not then require an additional 'alif like usual, e.g.

نبأً، مبدأً، إجراءً، مساءً

otherwise, the two *fatḥas* ً are followed by an 'alif ا e.g.

جزءًا، رزءًا

4. Writing and reading

1. At the beginning of a word

أُخْتٌ، أَبٌ، أُمٌّ، أَخذَ، أَكْرَمَ، أَمَلٌ، أَدَبٌ، أُذُنٌ، أَرْضٌ، أَرُزٌّ

2. In the middle or at the end of a word

سؤالٌ، اقـرئي جـاءَ، كُؤوسٌ، رَئيسٌ، لَئيمٌ، قِـراءَةٌ، شُرَكـاء، أَتَسَاءَلُ، طائِرٌ، طائِرَةٌ، كِبْرياء، إنْ شاءَ الله، مَسْؤول، رَأْسٌ، رَأَيْتُ، بُؤْسٌ، فُؤادٌ، مُتَفائِلٌ، تَأَخَّرْتُ، مَسْأَلَةٌ، بِئْر.

5. Review: *letters and words*

اِذْهَبْ go! اُكْتُبْ write!

إِمْرَأَة	woman
إِسْمي	my name
إِبْنَتي	my daughter
إِبْني	my son
إِثْنان	two
اَلْمَكْتَب	the office
إِسْتَخْرَجَ	he extracted
إِنْتَهى	he finished
إِنْفِجار	explosion
بابُ ٱلْمَكْتَب	the door of the office
ما ٱسْمُكَ؟	what is your name?
هذا ٱبْنُهُ	this is his son
قال: ٱمرَأَتي	he said: my wife
مَريضَة	is sick
قَرَأَ	he read
بَدَأَ	he began
ثَأْر	revenge
فَجأَة	suddenly
يَئِسَ	he gave up all hope
يُؤَدّي	something leads (to)
مُؤْمِن	faithful, believer
جُزْء	part
ضَوْء	light
بَدْء	beginning
ماء	water
سوء	evil

مَساء	evening
جاء	he came
وُضوء	ritual ablution
مروءَة	the ideal of manhood, esp., valor, chivalry, generosity, sense of honor
حَياء	timidity
توءمان	twin
مروءات	the ideals of manhood
إحصاءات	statistics
إجراءات	measures
نبأ	news item
مبدأ	principle
إجراء	performance (of an action), enforcement
أُخْت	sister
أَب	father
أُمّ	mother
أَخَذَ	he took
أَكْرَمَ	he honored (someone)
أَمَل	hope
أَدَب	literature
أُذُن	ear
سُؤال	question
إِقرئي	read! *fem.*

جاءَ	he came
كُؤوس	drinking glasses
رئيس	president
لئيم	mean, vile
قراءة	reading
شركاء	partners
أَتساءَل	I ask, wonder whether
طائِر	bird
طائرة	airplane
كبرياء	haughtiness, pride
إنْ شاءَ اللّه	if God wills, God willing
مسؤول	responsible
رأس	head
رَأَيْتُ	I saw
بُؤْس	misery
فُؤاد	heart, also a man's name
متفائِل	optimist
تَأَخَّرْتُ	I was late
مَسْأَلَة	question
بِئْر	well, spring

UNIT XII

1. Conversation

Review Lesson 1: *At The Airport* plus all dialogues in previous units.

2. Writing and reading

1. Fill in the blanks and read:

١ ـ اِسمي . . .

٢ ـ أنا من . . .

٣ ـ أنا طالب في
جامعة . . .
أنا طالبة في
جامعة . . .

٤ ـ أدرس اللغة العربية

٥ ـ عمري . . .

٦ ـ عنواني
شارع . . .
رقم . . .
مدينة . . .

٧ ـ رقم هاتفي . . .

2. Dictation: Write then read and translate.

أنا طالب في جامعة القاهرة. أدرس اللغة العربية، وعلم الاجتماع. عمري عشرون سنة. وأنا أعزب. أسكن مع صديق إنكليزي في شارع الجيزة، رقم ٩.

ولدت في مدينة سان فرانسيسكو لوالدين لبنانيين.
والدي طبيب، ووالدتي أستاذة في جامعة بيركلي.

كنت في زيارة قصيرة للبنان مع والديّ في **العام** year **الماضي** last .

Advances in mathematics enabled the Arabs to correct mistaken theories of earlier Greek and Indian astronomers. Caliph al-Mamun of Baghdad built observatories where his astronomers refined man's studies of the skies. They performed a delicate geodetic operation when they accurately measured the length of a terrestrial degree. Many astronomical terms used today, such as azimuth, nadir, and zenith, are Arabic.

3. Arabic words in the English language

There are about a thousand main words of Arabic origin in English and many thousand derivatives from those words. Many of the main words are rare nowadays, but some are still current in either technical or in everyday usage.

1. Read the following words and guess their meaning:

الكُحول - الجَبْر - الكيمياء - أميرال - أَمير - البُرْقوق - صِفْر - قُطْن - زرافَة - لَيْمون - مَخْزَن -

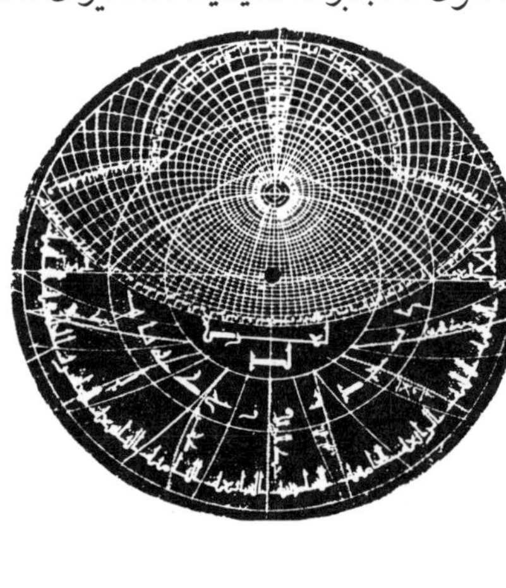

This astrolabe, with notations in Arabic, was based on research by Arab scholars first in mathematics, then in astronomy. Astrolabes were used by Arab sailors — and later by many European navigators and explorers — to ascertain a vessel's position at sea.

نارَنْج - شَراب - سُكَّر - تَعْريفَة - عود - رُزّ - قَهوة - الشاه مـات - زَعْفَران - قَنْـد - مكرمـة - أرضي
شوكي - كَمّون - حَشّاشين - بَلْسَم - كَـراوْيا - سَبـانخ - سِمْسِم - جَـرّة - وادي - المُناخ - الإنْبيق -
الإكسـير - سَمْت - المَلْغَم - البُوْرَق - قِـلْي - صَكّ -
عَنْـبر - الخَوارِزْمي - عِـطْر - قِرْمِـزي - ليلك -
دِمَشْق - رَباب - قيثار - رِزْمَة - طُنْبور - طَبْل.

اسطرلاب عربي

Arab pharmacists were highly respected members of the community. Their medicines included such common substances as alcohol, cassia, senna, arsenic, camphor, balsam, and borax. Bitter drugs were made more tasty by mixing them with syrups.

APPLICATION FORM

طلب عمل (استمارة)

1. Full name ______ ١ ـ الاسم والشهرة
   (Family name) ______ (اسم الأسرة، أو العائلة)
   (First name) ______ (الاسم الأول)

2. Date and place of birth ______ ٢ ـ تاريخ ومكان الولادة
   Day ______ اليوم
   Month ______ الشهر
   Year ______ السنة

3. Nationality ______ ٣ ـ الجنسية

4. Father's name ______ ٤ ـ اسم الأب
   Mother's name ______ اسم الأم

5. Present address ______ ٥ ـ مكان الإقامة الحالي
   Permanent address ______ العنوان الدائم
   Telephone number ______ رقم الهاتف
   Home ______ في البيت
   Work ______ في العمل

6. Occupation ______ ٦ ـ المهنة

7. Height ______ ٧ ـ الطول
   Weight ______ الوزن

Color ______ اللون

Eyes ______ العينان

Hair ______ الشعر

8. Marital status ______ الوضع العائلي ـ ٨

Single ______ أعزب

Married ______ متزوّج

Widower ______ أرمل

Divorced ______ مطلّق

9. Do you have children? ______ هل عندك أولاد؟ ـ ٩

Yes ______ نعم

No ______ لا

If 'Yes' please describe إذا كان الجواب «نعم» أكمل المعلومات التالية :

Date of birth ______ تاريخ الولادة

Name ______ الاسم

10. How many languages do you speak? ______

______ كم لغة تتكلم؟ ـ ١٠

What is your mother tongue? ______

______ ما هي لغة أمك الأصلية؟

What is your father tongue? ______

______ ما هي لغة أبيك الأصلية؟

Comprehend ______ فهم

Speak ______ كلام

Write ______ كتابة

Read ______ قراءة

Fluently ______ بطلاقة

With difficulty ____ الألمانية ____ بصعوبة

Other languages ____ اللغات الأخرى

---

11. Education ____ ١١ـ الثقافة .

Give full details ____ أُذكر التفاصيل الكاملة

Specialization ____ الكيمياء ____ الاختصاص

Degree ____ [illegible] ____ الشهادة

University ____ [illegible] ____ الجامعة

From year... ١٩٥٢ ، ١٩٧٧ ____ من سنة . . .

To year... ١٩٥٦ ، ١٩٧٩ ____ إلى سنة . . .

High school ____ المدرسة الثانوية

Kind of school ____ حكومية ____ نوع المدرسة

Name ____ المدرسة فلتن ____ الاسم

Address ____ العنوان

Country ____ أمريكية ____ البلد

---

12. List professional societies to which you belong ____

____

١٢ـ أُذكر أسماء الجمعيات التي تنتسب إليها ____

____

---

13. Employment record ____ ١٣ـ تاريخ العمل (التوظيف)

Present post ____ العمل الحالي

From... to ____ من . . . إلى

Month... year ____ شهر . . . سنة . . .

Salary ____ الراتب

Title of your position ____ اسم المركز الذي شغلته

Name of employer ____ اسم ربّ العمل

Address of employer ____ عنوان ربّ العمل

14. Have you ever been convicted? ______ ١٤ - هل حُكِمَ عليك؟

Yes ______ نعم

No ______ X ______ لا

If 'Yes' give full details ______

إذا كان الجواب «نعم» فاذكر التفاصيل ______

15. Signature ______ ١٥ - التوقيع

Date ______ التاريخ

بكالوريوس
baccalaureate

private (school) خاصّة
public (") حكومية

KEY TO EXERCISE 3 IN UNIT XII

Alcohol - algebra - alchemy - admiral - Emir - apricot - cipher - cotton - giraffe - lemon - magazine (as a store house) - orange - syrup - sugar - tariff - lute - rice - coffee - check-mate - saffron - candy - macramé - artichoke - cumin - assassin - balsam - caraway - spinach - sesame - jar - wadi - almanac - alembic - elixir - zenith - amalgam - borax - alkali - check - amber - algorism - attar - crimṣon - lilac - damask - rebec - guitar - ream - tambour - tabor

CROSSWORD PUZZLE

1.

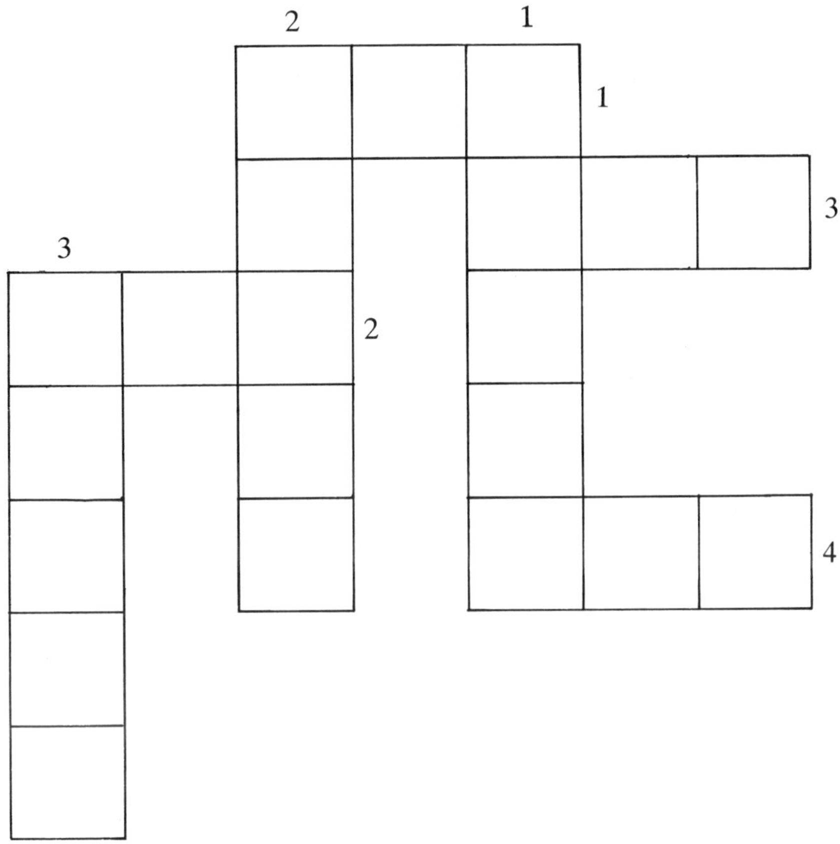

Across
1. Snow
2. Banana
3. Fire
4. House

Down
1. Talkative
2. University
3. A visit

2.

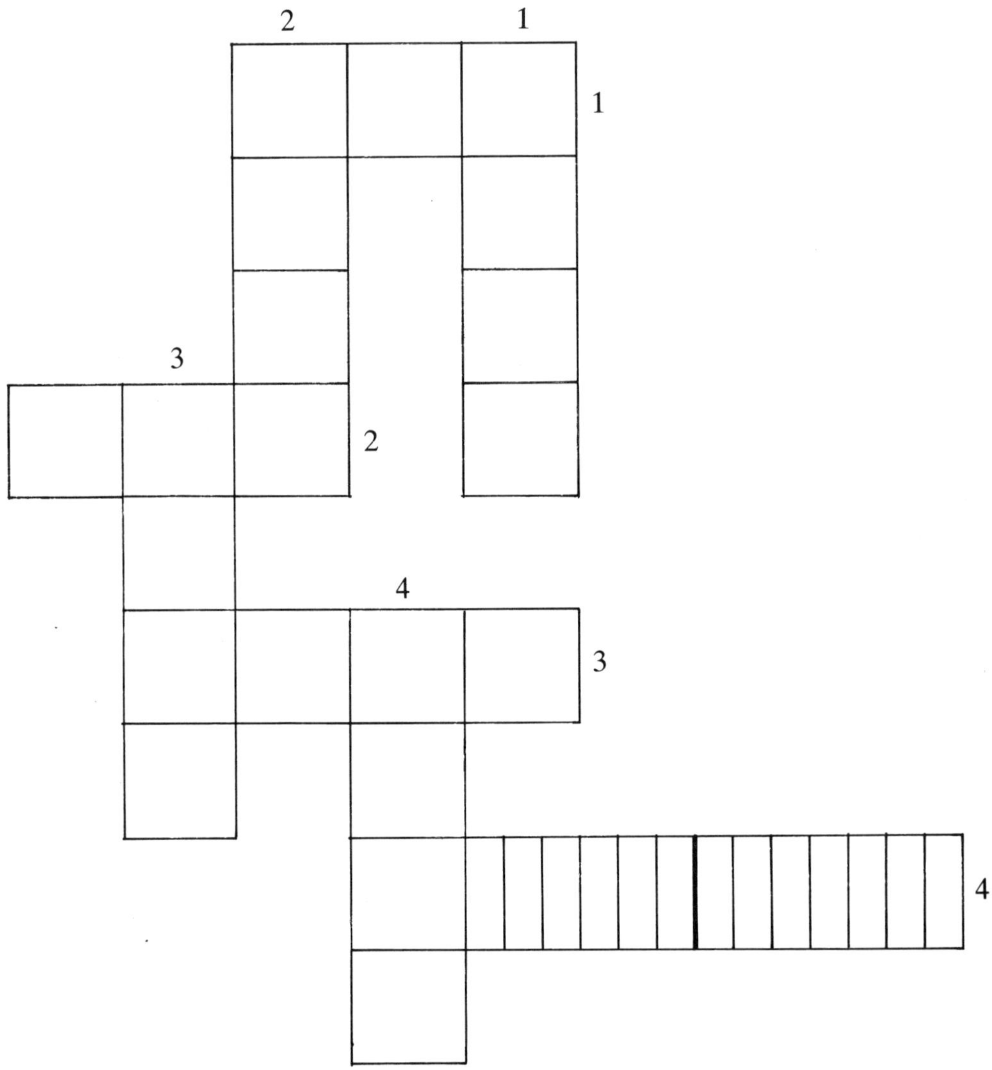

Across
1. Fish
2. Sea
3. Indian (from India)
4. Racial discrimination

Down
1. Bed
2. Book
3. Lover
4. Distinguished, eminent

SOLUTION TO PUZZLE 1

3		2		1			
		ج	ل	ث			1
		ا		ر		ن	3
ز	ء	م	2	ث			
ي		ع		ا			
ا		ة		ر	ا	د	4
ر							
ة							

SOLUTION TO PUZZLE 2

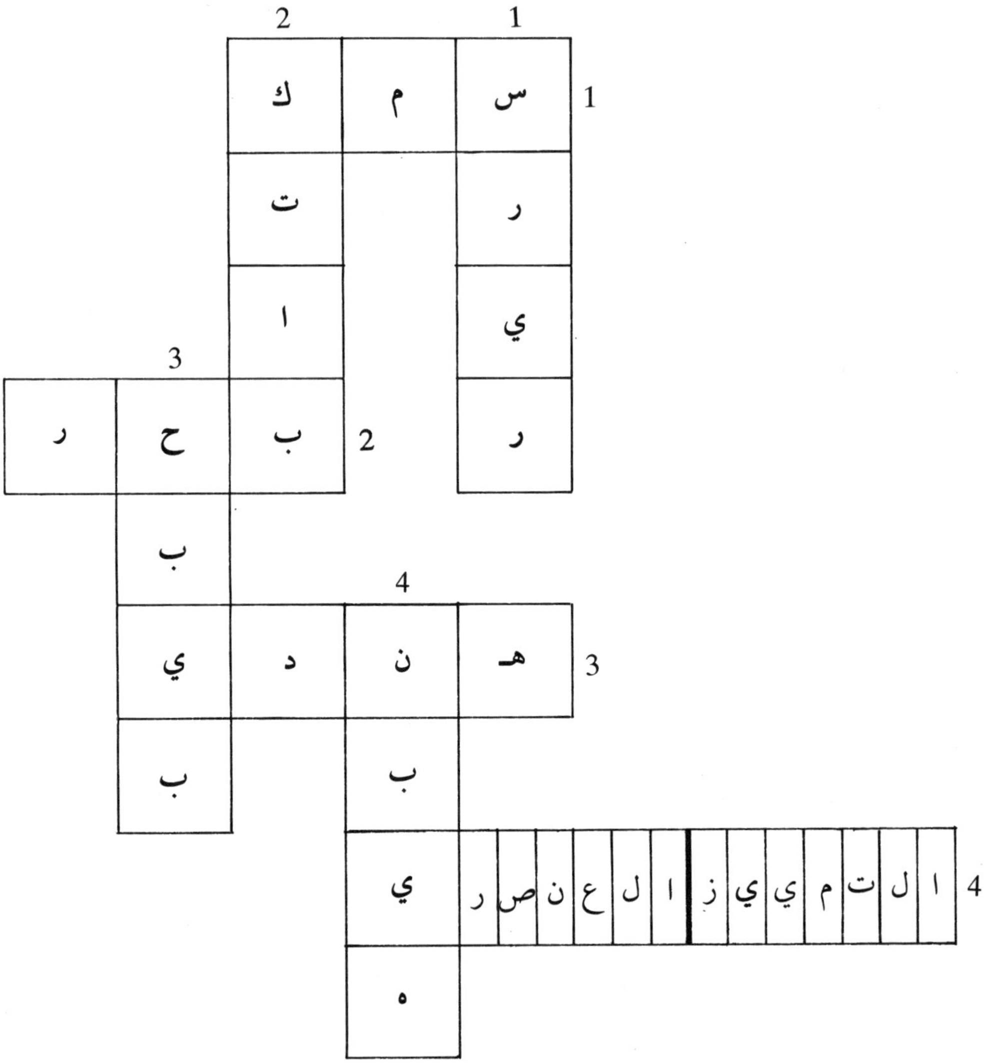